As the financial crisis continues to cast
rope, the view that immigrants compete ui
an unsustainable burden on the Europeai.   ..... uppcaio to
be gathering support in some circles. At the same time, the 'right'
type of immigrant has often been perceived as a potential cure for
Europe's sluggish labour markets and ailing welfare systems –
especially immigrants who are young, easily employable and who
arrive without family. So far, efforts to solve this conundrum – as
in the UK's points-based system – have focused on increasing the
selectivity of the admissions process. In this book, leading immigration experts question the effectiveness of this approach. Besides efforts
to regulate the flow and rights of immigrants, they argue that governments across Europe need to devise labour market, welfare and
immigration policies in a more integrated fashion.

Edited by Elena Jurado and Grete Brochmann

europe's immigration challenge

Reconciling Work, Welfare and Mobility

I.B. TAURIS

LONDON · NEW YORK

Published in 2013 by I.B.Tauris & Co Ltd
6 Salem Road, London W2 4BU
175 Fifth Avenue, New York NY 10010
www.ibtauris.com

Distributed in the United States and Canada Exclusively by Palgrave Macmillan
175 Fifth Avenue, New York NY 10010

ISBN: 978 1 78076 225 8 (HB)
ISBN: 978 1 78076 226 5 (PB)

A full CIP record for this book is available from the British Library
A full CIP record is available from the Library of Congress

Library of Congress Catalog Card Number: available

Typeset in Minion by MPS Limited
Printed and bound in Great Britain by T.J. International, Padstow, Cornwall

About Policy Network

Policy Network is a leading thinktank and international political network based in London. We seek to promote strategic thinking on progressive solutions to the challenges of the twenty-first century and the future of social democracy, impacting upon policy debates in the UK, the rest of Europe and the wider world.

We organise debates and conduct research on policy and political challenges that present all governments and political parties with urgent dilemmas, either because sustainable solutions remain elusive, or because there are political barriers to their implementation.

Through a distinctly collaborative and cross-national approach to research, events and publications, we have acquired a reputation as a highly valued platform for perceptive and challenging political analysis, debate and exchange. Building from our origins in the late 1990s, the network has become an unrivalled international point-of-contact between political thinkers and opinion formers, serving as a nexus between the worlds of politics, academia, public policy-making, business, civil society and the media.

www.policy-network.net

Contents

Acknowledgements   *ix*

Contributors   *xi*

Introduction: Immigration, Work and Welfare: Towards
an Integrated Approach   1
Elena Jurado, Grete Brochmann and Jon Erik Dølvik

1   Migration and the Political Economy of the
Welfare State: Thirty Years Later   15
Gary P. Freeman

2   European Movements of Labour: Challenges
for European Social Models   33
Jon Erik Dølvik

3   Migration and Welfare Sustainability:
The Case of Norway   59
Grete Brochmann and Anne Skevik Grødem

4   Immigration in Italy: Subverting the Logic of
Welfare Reform?   77
Giuseppe Sciortino

5   Responding to Employers: Skills, Shortages
and Sensible Immigration Policy   95
Martin Ruhs and Bridget Anderson

6   European Employers and the Rediscovery
of Labour Migration   105
Georg Menz

7   Long-Term Care and Migrant Labour in the UK   125
    Isabel Shutes

8   Irregular Immigration and the Underground
    Economy in Southern Europe: Breaking the
    Vicious Circle   143
    Emilio Reyneri

9   Restricting the Right to Family Migration
    in Denmark: When Human Rights Collide
    with a Welfare State under Pressure   159
    Emily Cochran Bech and Per Mouritsen

10 Migration, Immigration Controls and
    the Fashioning of Precarious Workers   185
    Bridget Anderson

Index   205

Acknowledgements

The rationale for this book originated from two programmes of research and seminars on labour migration organised by Policy Network in 2008–9, with the generous support of the Barrow Cadbury Trust. The programmes brought together scholars, policy-makers and other stakeholders from across Europe to discuss the economic impacts of immigration and consider the changes needed to the immigration policies of individual European countries in order to maximise the benefits of immigration and minimise its costs. However, the seminars organised in the context of this research programme quickly brought to light the limitations of this traditional approach. In particular, it became evident that, if immigration was to have win–win results for immigrant and non-immigrant populations alike, changes would be necessary not only to European immigration policies, but also to some of Europe's most cherished labour-market and welfare institutions.

We would like to extend our warmest thanks to Sara Llewellin, Chief Executive, and Ayesha Saran, Programme Manager, at the Barrow Cadbury Trust whose sponsorship and intellectual support made the seminar series possible. We are also grateful to the wonderful team at Policy Network who helped to make the seminars a success and contributed at various stages to the preparation of the book. In this context, we would like to mention Annie Bruzzone and Arjun Singh-Muchelle whose enthusiasm and interest in the migration conundrum helped us to refine the ideas which run through this book. Anita Hurrell, Nabeelah Jaffer and in particular Michael McTernan were instrumental in the editing and production process and we thank them for the diligence and professionalism with which they carried out these tasks.

Last but not least, we are indebted to Olaf Cramme, Roger Liddle and Patrick Diamond for their continuous support and for creating the stimulating intellectual environment upon which Policy Network continues to thrive.

Elena Jurado and Grete Brochmann
London and Oslo

Contributors

Bridget Anderson is Professor of Migration and Citizenship and Deputy Director at the Centre on Migration, Policy and Society (COMPAS), University of Oxford. Her main fields of research are citizenship and belonging, low-waged labour markets, and domestic labour. She is author of *Doing the Dirty Work? The global politics of domestic labour* (Zed Books, 2000). She also co-edited with Martin Ruhs, *Who Needs Migrant Workers? Labour shortages, immigration and public policy.* Her book, *Us and Them? The dangerous politics of immigration control,* will be published by OUP in 2013.

Emily Cochran Bech is a PhD candidate in political science at Columbia University, and currently a visiting PhD scholar at the Department of Political Science and Government in Aarhus University. Her main fields of research are in national and group identities in politics, immigrant civic identity and political participation, Muslim organisations' political engagement in Western Europe, and the political and social effects of the ethnicisation of Muslims in Western democracies.

Grete Brochmann is Professor of Sociology and Head of the Department of Sociology and Human Geography at the University of Oslo. She has published several books and articles on International migration, sending and receiving country perspectives, EU policies, welfare state dilemmas as well as historical studies on immigration. She has served as a visiting scholar in Brussels, Berkeley and Boston. In 2002 she held the Willy Brandt Guest Professorship in Malmö, Sweden. She was recently head of a governmental commission on International Migration and the Norwegian Welfare Model.

Jon Erik Dølvik is Head of Research at the Fafo Institute for Labour and Social Research in Oslo. His main field of research is comparative, European employment relations and labour-market governance. He has in recent years published extensively on issues related to European integration and labour migration.

Gary P. Freeman is Professor and Chair of the Department of Government at the University of Texas at Austin. He specialises in the politics of immigration, comparative social policy and politics in Western democracies. His books include *Immigrant Labor and Racial Conflict in Industrial Societies, Nations of Immigrants: Australia, the United States and International Migration* (edited with James Jupp), *Immigration Policy and Security: US, European, and Commonwealth Perspectives* (edited with Terri Givens and David Leal), and *Immigration and Public Opinion in Liberal Democracies* (edited with Randall Hansen and David Leal).

Anne Skevik Grødem is Sociologist and Researcher at Fafo Institute of Labour and Social Research. She was a central member of the secretariat to the Norwegian Welfare and Migration Committee (2009–2011). Her main research interests are welfare policy, family sociology, poverty and social exclusion.

Elena Jurado is Senior Consultant at ICF GHK, an international research consultancy which offers services to private and public sector clients across the whole policy, programme and project cycle, including research, evaluations and impact assessments, as well as implementation. At ICF GHK, Elena manages projects and works as an expert in the areas of migration and asylum, employment, and social policy. Between 2007 and 2011, Elena was Head of Research at Policy Network. Previously, she worked in the minorities unit of the Council of Europe and as a Politics lecturer at the University of Oxford.

Georg Menz is Professor of Political Economy and Jean Monnet Chair in European Integration at Goldsmiths College, University of London. He is the author of *The Political Economy of Managed Migration* (2008) and *Varieties of Capitalism and Europeanization* as well as numerous journal articles on questions of immigration, social and labour market policy, and international political economy.

Per Mouritsen is Lecturer in Political Theory at the Department of Political Science, University of Aarhus. His primary research interests are migration studies, classical and modern political theory, republicanism, tolerance and multiculturalism, citizenship and public service. He has held central positions in several international projects under the 6th EU Framework Program EMILIE concerning European perspectives on citizenship and multiculturalism. His list of publications include titles such as: *The Fragility of Liberty: A Reconstruction of Republican Citizenship* (2001), and *Constituting Communities: Political Solutions to Cultural Conflict* (with Knud Erik Jørgensen, 2008).

Emilio Reyneri is Professor in the Department of Sociology and Social Research at the University of Milan Bicocca. A Member of the Scientific Council of Journals of Economic and Labour Sociology, he was part of the Commission for Integration at the Italian government's Department of Social Affairs. His research interests focus on the various forms of unemployment in European countries, atypical work, the structure of employment by professional levels, the ways of regulating the labour market, labour policies, the relationship between illegal immigration and the economy, the penalisation of immigrant workers in receiving labour markets, and relations between sociological and economic analysis of the labour market.

Martin Ruhs is University Lecturer in Political Economy at Oxford University's Department for Continuing Education, a Fellow of Kellogg College, and Senior Research Fellow at the Centre on Migration, Policy and Society (COMPAS).

Giuseppe Sciortino teaches Sociology at the Università di Trento, Italy. He has published widely in migration studies and cultural sociology. His most recent works include, *Great Minds. Encounters with Social Theory* (Stanford, 2011, with Gianfranco Poggi) and *Foggy Social Structures: Irregular Migration, European Labour Markets and the Welfare State* (Amsterdam UP, 2011, edited with Michael Bommes).

Isabel Shutes is Lecturer in Social Policy at the London School of Economics and Political Science. She has research interests in welfare states and migration; social divisions and inequalities; social care; and relations between the state, market and third sector.

Introduction
Immigration, Work and Welfare: Towards an Integrated Approach

Elena Jurado, Grete Brochmann and Jon Erik Dølvik

As the global financial crisis plunged Europe into a prolonged recession in 2009, public attitudes to immigration, already sceptical during the economic upturn, hardened perceptibly. A Transatlantic Trends survey conducted in six European countries in the same year found that the number of people describing immigration as 'more of a problem than an opportunity' had increased by seven percentage points on the previous year, representing 50 per cent of the population.[1] While public attitudes are influenced by a multitude of factors, the crisis has evidently played a role, as the same survey found that families who experienced financial difficulties in the past 12 months tended to be more worried about immigration than those whose financial situation had stayed the same or improved. Today, although levels of hostility towards immigrants appear to have stabilised, anti-immigrant sentiment continues to stand at record levels in many European countries.[2]

For large sectors of the European public, at a time of high unemployment and budget constraints, Europe cannot afford to further open its doors to immigrants who will add to 'low-pay job competition' and present a 'burden on our welfare systems'. At the same time, the 'right' type of immigrant has long been perceived by employers and governments as a potential cure for Europe's sluggish labour markets and ailing welfare states – especially immigrants who are young and highly skilled and who arrive without family. Although the current economic downturn has somewhat stalled the 'global battle for talent', with a number of European governments increasing even the barriers to high-skilled immigration, there is a widespread perception that, in contrast to low-skilled workers, skills shortages in certain sectors of the European economy mean a growing supply of high-skilled workers is required during the period of economic contraction, and will certainly be required during the recovery.

Governments have sought to resolve this dilemma by toughening their discourse on immigration while setting limits on the numbers and types of immigrants who cross our borders; that is, by introducing more selective immigration policies which 'fast track' entry for high-skilled immigrants, while restricting the entry of those deemed 'economic burdens', including low-skilled migrants, family migrants and asylum-seekers. These skill-selective immigration policies have come in two main forms: immigrant-driven policies, where points are allocated to individual immigrants on the basis of particular attributes (usually a mixture of education, age and income); and employer-driven policies, where employers must sponsor the application for the admission of a foreign worker and typically need to carry out a 'labour market test'.

So far, the UK is the only European country that has introduced an explicit 'points-based system', enabling high-skilled migrants to gain entry without sponsorship from an employer.[3] Most other European countries, including Germany, Denmark and France, follow the second model and make residence permits available to immigrants who receive specific job offers with a yearly salary above a particular, pre-defined threshold. The EU has endeavoured to bolster these skill-selective immigration policies through the adoption in 2009 of a 'Blue Card' system, which aims to facilitate temporary access to the European labour market to highly qualified third-country nationals.[4] In all of these cases the underlying logic is the same: if only governments could find ways of attracting 'useful' immigrants to our borders while keeping 'unwanted' immigrants out, Europe's immigration conundrum would be solved.

One of the themes running through this book is that governments overestimate the control they have over the movement of people. In fact, the great majority of immigrants crossing EU borders, including EU citizens, people seeking international protection and irregular migrants, fall outside of, or manage to avoid, immigration controls. However, the book's main underlying concern is that current efforts to select immigrants according to their value to the economy underestimate the complexity of the relationship between migrant flows, labour markets and welfare systems. The value that immigrants bring to an economy, and the impact they may have on employment and public services, depends not only on the numbers and characteristics of the immigrants themselves, but also on the labour-market and welfare structures they enter.

While European countries share a common vision of society that combines sustainable economic growth with a high level of social security (the so-called 'European Social Model'), they use very different combinations of labour-market and welfare instruments to achieve this end. The result is what observers have described as three different European social models. First, a social-democratic or 'Nordic' model, featuring high levels of taxes, social expenditures and universal welfare provision, along with coordinated collective bargaining, strong labour unions and well-regulated labour markets, which ensure compressed wage structures. Second, a liberal or 'Anglo-Saxon' model, which has much looser employment protection legislation; a patchy, decentralised bargaining system; weaker unions; and work-first-oriented, residual welfare policies, resulting in comparatively high disparities in wages. And third, a conservative or 'Continental' model, where insurance-based benefits and strict employment-protection legislation for labour-market 'insiders' are combined with a strong 'male bread-winner' tradition. Although union membership is in decline in most countries, unions and collective bargaining systems remain strong in Nordic and several continental countries, where social partners are often included in processes of political decision-making and implementation.[5]

These different social models are today confronting multiple challenges. Principal among these are the process of demographic ageing and the decline of manufacturing in favour of a service economy – two developments that, alongside surging unemployment, have added to government welfare expenditure at a time when increased globalisation and European integration have arguably reduced government capacity to finance this spending by raising taxes. The result has been a wave of reforms aimed for the most part at the partial liberalisation of employment protection regulations, intended to raise the flexibility and effectiveness of Europe's sluggish labour markets. Other reforms have included welfare cuts and 'activation' measures aimed at reducing the number of welfare dependants and increasing employment and revenues. The current European debt crisis and the EU response to it have exacerbated such trends by forcing countries to adopt further retrenchment measures in order to stabilise spiralling budget deficits.

Immigration is a factor in these economic and political convulsions. Although a number of European countries have been net importers of labour since the 1960s, for many others, high levels of inward migration are a relatively new phenomenon. The large outflows of migrants from the 10 new accession countries following the 2004 and 2007 rounds of EU enlargement represented an important landmark in this respect, raising fears about Eastern European workers taking jobs, undercutting wages and undermining labour protections in the old member states. In their efforts to manage these welfare and migration challenges, the 'semi-sovereign welfare states'[6] in the EU/EEA are strongly interdependent. The EU's multi-level governance system includes an expanding body of European regulations governing social and labour-market policy and a 'dual' migration system. This 'dual' migration regime provides EU and EFTA nationals with the right to free movement across internal borders (31 EU/EFTA countries) and is gradually developing common policies towards third-country nationals.[7] The resulting divergence between the rights of EU nationals and third-country nationals implies a close interplay between EU internal and external migration flows and policies, where those countries who receive most EU migrants (like UK and Norway) will tend to adopt stricter policies vis-à-vis third-country nationals, while those who receive few EU migrants will seek to attract more third-country immigrants.[8]

In his pioneering essay on *Migration and the Political Economy of the Welfare State*, published in 1986, Gary Freeman warned about the corrosive effect of 'mass immigration' on the European welfare state.[9] He argued, first, that immigrants would undermine the position of native workers by doing work and accepting wages below European standards. Second, he warned that, by increasing cultural diversity within European states, immigration would erode the normative consensus on which generous welfare systems are based. More than 25 years after the publication of his essay, Freeman's arguments continue to resonate strongly with European political elites and public opinion alike. In recognition of this legacy, the present volume opens with a retrospective by Gary Freeman, where he defends the continuing relevance of the ideas he expounded in *Migration and the Political Economy of the Welfare State*. While a number of authors have found evidence to support Gary Freeman's claims, a growing body of researchers has highlighted problems with his argument. These researchers recognise the challenges that immigrants present to the sustainability of European welfare systems. However, they argue that Freeman's analysis overlooks the 'institutional repertoires' of the welfare state which structure the impact of immigration and diversity.[10]

This volume juxtaposes Gary Freeman's retrospective with eight essays by authors who investigate the way immigration interacts with the 'institutional repertoires' of the welfare state in a selection of countries with different social models. In doing so, they acknowledge that immigration flows, labour markets and welfare systems influence each other in a multitude of ways and cannot be analysed in isolation. Most of the authors explore this dynamic through individual country studies, but others have chosen to compare the impact of such dynamics across European countries. While identifying similarities across the national experiences, the chapters mostly serve to highlight variations in what are basically country-specific outcomes. In the remainder of this introduction we briefly review each of these essays before turning, in a concluding section, to sketch the implications of the nexus between migration, welfare and labour markets for policymaking.

Migration and the 'Rescue' of the European Social Model

Jon Erik Dølvik begins the European country analyses with a discussion of the effects of intra-EU migration on the current challenges facing the European social models. While EU migrants in principle enjoy equal treatment in the labour-market and social-security systems of other Member States, this right is not extended to workers 'posted' by European enterprises to work temporarily in another member state. For these workers, host countries can only require enterprises to comply with a core list of nationally defined working conditions, which recent judgments of the European Court of Justice have interpreted as an exhaustive, maximum list, including minimum rates of pay set by legislation or extended collective agreements. While acknowledging the impacts that increased migration and the posting of workers is having on the labour markets of EU Member States, including changes in company hiring practices which make it harder for trade unions to ensure proper conditions, the author situates these changes within a more general restructuring trend taking place in EU Member States over the past 15 years. This includes more project-based organisations, outsourcing and contractual flexibility, leading to increased segmentation and sharper divisions between the labour-market 'core' and 'periphery'. The interplay between growing intra-EU labour transfers, the erosion of labour-market regulations and high unemployment tends to accentuate such dualist dynamics in several sectors of the European economy.

The challenges presented by the interplay between generous social benefits, high minimum standards in the labour market and low-skilled migration are explored by Grete Brochmann and Anne Skevik Grødem in the next chapter of the book. As the authors explain, the Norwegian welfare state is universalistic in the sense of requiring comparatively short residence and/or employment periods for immigrants to gain access to most social benefits, including social assistance, disability, unemployment and sickness. Norway is also characterised by a well-regulated labour market, in particular, a compressed wage structure, the result of strong trade unions and coordinated collective bargaining. For decades, this system was praised for helping Norway maintain some of Europe's lowest unemployment rates. Today, however, many are questioning its sustainability in the face of growing numbers of immigrants. As the authors point out, such a model may end up attracting the type of immigration (low-skilled, low-productivity) which can challenge the basic structure of the model itself. On the one hand, Norway's compressed wage structure makes it difficult for low-skilled migrants to access the labour market. On the other hand, for low-skilled migrants who increasingly have to compete for low-paid work, Norway's generous benefits can create disincentives for low-skilled workers (who often include immigrants) to enter the labour market – the so-called 'welfare-trap'. Such dynamics can in the longer term undermine the high participation rates required to fund the extensive welfare system.

In the next chapter of the book, Giuseppe Sciortino explores the interrelationship between immigration flows, employment outcomes and a conservative welfare system. By relying on social insurance, Italy's welfare state makes social benefits dependent on previous work performance and is therefore strongly worker-oriented. In his analysis, Sciortino identifies a mutually reinforcing relationship between immigration and Italy's conservative welfare system, one that is helping to sustain a welfare regime that is increasingly at odds with Italy's changing social reality. As more and more women join the labour market, the system's emphasis on monetary transfers over the provision of services has created an insatiable demand for unskilled foreign labour to provide the childcare and long-term care services to private households that the state is unable to afford. While the informal interplay between Italy's conservative welfare regime and unskilled immigration flows enables Italian society to function in the short-term, Sciortino warns that it has constrained the ability of Italian policymakers to plan the flows of new workers, and has helped to delay the adoption of labour-market and welfare reforms needed in order to ensure the long-term competitiveness of Italy's economy. Indeed, with foreign labour over-represented in the low-skilled, low-wage jobs which most Italian citizens continue to spurn, there has been little incentive to reform the ever sharper divisions between Italy's labour market 'core' and 'periphery'.

The relationship between immigration and the UK's 'liberal' social model is explored by Martin Ruhs and Bridget Anderson. In their joint chapter for this volume, they show how the weakly regulated construction industry in the UK has resulted in a predominance of temporary, project-based work, informal recruitment and casualised employment and an over-representation of migrant workers.

This in turn has helped to encourage employers to pursue low-cost, low-productivity corporate strategies, which has eroded their incentive to invest in long-term training. In his overview of the factors which shape employer preferences toward migration, Georg Menz makes a similar point, contrasting vocational training in the UK, which relies on individualised, company-specific skills and 'on the job training' with Germany's comprehensive education and training system, which produces highly specialised 'sectorally portable' skills capable of sustaining Germany's high-value-added export strategies. For Menz, these contrasting systems go a long way in explaining why German employers have lobbied hard for Germany's immigration policy to focus entirely on highly skilled, high-wage labour, while British employers maintain a more 'liberal' approach, lobbying government to open immigration routes for both high-skilled and low-skilled workers.

The contrast between Germany and the UK also serves to highlight another important linkage between immigration and Europe's different social models. It is not only the low-cost strategies pursued by employers in the UK's deregulated labour market that explains the greater influx of low-skilled migrants into the UK. The UK's 'minimalist' social security system, where benefits in kind, such as the provision of long-term care, childcare and public housing, are means-tested also means that low-skilled migrants simply represent less of an economic 'threat' than they might in Norway or Germany. In her chapter, Isabel Shutes provides a stark warning of the effects that such a system can have on both the quality of public services and the employment conditions of public service workers. In her analysis of the UK's long-term care sector, Shutes shows how the wages and employment conditions of workers in private sector long-term care services tend to be lower than the wages and conditions of workers in long-term care services managed by public or not-for-profit institutions. For Shutes it is no coincidence that foreign labour is over-represented in private sector long-term care, since foreign workers are often more willing to work longer shifts for lower wages as a result of the precarity of their immigration status. She concludes that it is the interaction between the UK's welfare arrangements for older people – which have undergone considerable privatisation in recent years – and the UK's immigration rules that creates sub-optimal employment outcomes for immigrants and, ultimately, downward pressures on wages and conditions for all workers in the sector.

The last three chapters focus on the efforts of countries belonging to the three different social models to implement skill-selective immigration policies. In his detailed analysis of the connections between irregular immigration and the underground economy in Southern European countries, Emilio Reyneri explains that the quota systems that prevail in these countries, based on employer sponsorship of individual immigrants prior to their arrival, are rendered useless. These quotas are unable to meet the strong demand for low-skilled labour stemming from Southern European countries' reliance on low-skilled labour intensive sectors, especially agriculture, construction and domestic care for private households, which the local workforce refuses to carry out. As Reyneri explains, workers in these sectors are normally hired on the basis of personal attitudes and face-to-face selection, and vacancies are therefore difficult to fill using a quota system, where employers must sponsor individual workers before they cross the border on the basis of a CV and other formal requirements. The weakness of existing channels for recruiting low-skilled foreign labour in Southern Europe is a large part of the explanation for the large stock of irregular migrants that exist in these countries.

In their chapter on Denmark, Emily Cochran Bech and Per Mouritsen likewise show that attempts to restrict family migration in order to 'rescue' the Danish welfare state may be having a number of perverse effects. In 2010, Denmark's family migration policies – already some of the most stringent in Europe – were tightened further with the introduction of a new exam and point system requiring the foreign-resident spouse to have 'integration-relevant qualifications', including Danish language competency, education qualifications and work experience, with further language and civic requirements imposed on the Danish-resident spouse. In the short-run, the new policies did substantially reduce the number of family migrants entering Denmark. However, the authors show that the policies did not increase the number of interracial marriages and there is evidence that they may be dissuading economic migrants from settling in Denmark. More perversely, they come into conflict with international and European human rights conventions, which limit state autonomy in legislating family migration rules regarding refugees, EU migrants and even third-country nationals living within a state's territory. As a result, Denmark's selective approach to family migration may end up affecting only the family reunification requests of Danish citizens, with the people whose family reunification Danish legislators want to influence remaining beyond reach.

Even in the UK, with its more sophisticated points-based system, policymakers have been unable to ensure that immigration policies are fit for purpose. As Bridget Anderson shows in her chapter for this volume, only those immigrants who qualify to enter under Tier 1 (high-skilled migrants) can do so on the basis of points, without sponsorship from an employer. All other immigrants who enter under Tier 2 (skilled) or Tier 3 (low-skilled) must have a 'certificate of sponsorship'.[11] Anderson shows how this bureaucratic and complex system of control, which makes skilled and unskilled foreign workers dependent on their employer for legal status, is perversely responsible for the state losing control over migration. Caught between inflexible immigration rules, such as the prohibition on moving from one employer to another, and a labour market that is weakly regulated, unskilled foreign workers in the UK easily descend into illegality. In doing so, they not only exacerbate the precarity of the foreign workers; by combining with the UK's weakly regulated labour market, they also undermine the position of the native-born workforce by creating a 'race to the bottom' in wages and employment standards in segments of the labour market which rely on high shares of migrant labour.

Policy Implications

The efforts of each country analysed in this book to implement skill-selective immigration policies are constrained, and often undermined, by their failure to take into account the actual dynamics of the welfare systems and labour markets they are embedded in. Besides efforts to improve admissions policy, governments need to give greater consideration to the way that labour-market regulation and welfare policies influence not only demand for foreign labour, but also the economic and social incorporation of immigrant and non-immigrant groups. When thinking about the strategies that governments should adopt, it is clear that there can be no one-size-fits all solutions. The challenges that emerge from the interaction between immigration, labour markets and welfare systems are specific to each social model and the solutions to these must therefore be tailored to the particular situation each country is in, while taking into account their common embeddedness in EU institutions and regulations.

Europe requires innovative immigration policies which recognise not only the demand for skills in different sectors of the economy, but also the impact that immigrants can have on important labour-market and welfare institutions. In certain countries, like Italy, where small-scale, often low-productivity industries dominate the labour market, one option could be to open up more channels for low-skilled labour to prevent employers from having to recruit migrants 'off the books'. In other countries, like Norway, where comparatively high minimum wages and productivity requirements can make it hard for migrants to gain access to employment, a greater emphasis on language, skill formation and vocational training seems necessary to strengthen the employability of the new migrant labour force. In the UK, immigration policies need to be complemented by measures that ensure immigrants, especially the less skilled, more rights and protection in order to prevent their dependency on often-abusive employers and a growing precarity of immigrant labour.

Labour-market policies will also need adjustment in light of the growing levels of immigration. Most importantly, measures are required to ensure a proper wage floor and a minimum set of employment protections for all workers. In some countries, such as Norway, these institutions exist but are being subject to erosion by employer circumvention, enforcement problems and the difficulties which trade unions often face in striking agreements and organising in companies predominantly hiring migrant labour. For trade unions, their increasingly diverse constituencies require innovative approaches to promote recruitment and influence in the multi-ethnic service sector in particular. In other countries, such as the UK, with fragmented bargaining systems and liberalised employment protection, the rise in casual, low-paid work among migrants accentuates the case for re-embedding and re-regulation of the labour market. In conservative welfare regimes, such as Italy's, where labour markets are segmented between a set of 'core' workers, who enjoy high levels of protection, and those on the 'periphery', who do not, the challenge is to find proper ways of overcoming this segmentation.

For the ailing European welfare systems, the rise in immigration represents both opportunity and challenge. In order to reap the benefits of an increased supply of migrant labour, the contributions in this volume highlight the need for comprehensive approaches, linking immigration policies with social and labour-market policies. This is as true for countries with social democratic welfare models as it is for countries with conservative or liberal welfare systems. Variations in the degree of and basis for welfare coverage – universal, insurance-based or means-tested – are less important than the ability of governments to develop social services and benefit systems that are capable of enhancing labour-market participation and skill formation and creating minimum wage setting systems that 'make work pay'. As long as these pre-conditions are in place, immigration can contribute to 'double gains' by providing both the labour and revenues needed to sustain the European welfare states.

Notes

1. See Transatlantic Trends: Immigration, 2009. http://trends.gmfus. org/files/archived/immigration/doc/TTI_2009_Key.pdf. The six European countries included in the survey are: Italy, Germany, France, Netherlands, Spain and the United Kingdom.
2. Transatlantic Trends: Immigration, 2011. http://trends.gmfus. org/files/2011/12/TTImmigration_final_web.pdf.
3. Variations on this points-based system have long existed in the USA, Canada, Australia and New Zealand.

4. The EU's 'Blue Card Directive' establishes common broad criteria – based on a minimum salary level – to qualify for admission. However, it has been criticised as too limited in scope, in particular, for its failure to ensure coordination between Member States in the setting of specific admissions criteria. See for example Cerna, L. 'The EU Blue Card. A Bridge Too far?' Paper prepared for the Fifth Pan-European Conference on EU Politics Porto, Portugal 23–26 June, 2010.

5. In fact, the literature distinguishes other models as well, including a 'Mediterranean' and an 'East European' model, but these are essentially variants of one of the three main models mentioned here. See especially Esping-Andersen, G. *The Three World's of Welfare Capitalism.* Cambridge: Polity Press, 1990. See also Hall, P. and Soskice, D. (eds). *Varieties of Capitalism: The Institutional Foundations of Comparative Advantage.* Oxford: Oxford University Press, 2001; and Sapir, A. 'Globalisation and the Reform of European Social Models'. *Bruegel Policy Brief,* Issue 2005/01, November 2005.

6. Leibfried, S. and Pierson, P. 'Semi-Sovereign Welfare States: Social Policy in a Multi-tiered Europe'. In S. Leibfried and P. Pierson (eds) *European Social Policy: Between Fragmentation and Integration.* Washington, DC: The Brookings Institute, 1995.

7. In addition to the above-mentioned 'Blue Card Directive', adopted by the EU in May 2009, the EU has recently also adopted the so-called 'Single Permit Directive', which provides a common set of rights for all non-EU workers that have already been admitted but have not been provided long-term resident status. The EU is currently debating two further Directives, one on seasonal workers and another on intra-corporate transfers of non-EU skilled workers. For an overview of the EU's evolving policy towards third-country nationals see Olsson, P. H. *Giving to Those Who Have and Taking From Those Who Have Not – The Development of an EU Policy on Workers from Third Countries.* Formula Working Paper, no. 34, 2012.

8. According to EU free movement rules, Member States shall in principle give primacy to intra-EU labour migration, and third-country labour migration is only warranted if vacancies cannot be filled by EU/EEA-citizens. For a comprehensive overview of the EU's 'dual' migration regime, and the migration dynamics it has generated, see Boswell, C. and Geddes, A. *Migration and Mobility in the European Union*. Basingstoke: Palgrave Macmillan, 2010.

9. Freeman, G. P. 'Migration and the Political Economy of the Welfare State'. *The Annals of the American Academy of Political and Social Science*, 485/1 (1986): 51–63.

10. See in particular Bommes, M. and Geddes, A. (eds). *Immigration and Welfare: Challenging the Borders of the Welfare State*. New York: Routledge, 2002; Banting, K. and Kymlicka, W. (eds). *Multiculturalism and the welfare state. Recognition and Redistribution in Contemporary Democracies*. Oxford: Oxford University Press, 2006; and Crepaz, M. M. *Trust beyond Borders. Immigration, the Welfare State, and Identity in Modern Societies*. Ann Arbor: University of Michigan Press, 2008.

11. Tier 3, however, has remained closed since the launch of the new immigration system.

CHAPTER 1

Migration and the Political Economy of the Welfare State: Thirty Years Later

Gary P. Freeman

Sometime in 1985 I sat down with a yellow legal pad and a pencil (personal computers had not yet entered my life) and in a couple of hours sketched out the main contours of a paper that was subsequently presented to no great fanfare at the annual meeting of the International Studies Association in Washington, DC. The paper was duly published in a special issue of the *Annals of the American Academy of Political and Social Science*, edited by Martin Heisler and Barbara Schmitter Heisler.[1]

The ideas in the paper were provoked as much by my forebodings after observing and writing about immigration and the welfare state for more than a decade as by hard data. My personal biography included growing up in the Deep South in the era of segregation and watching at close hand the unfolding of the civil rights movement. Immigrants played only a small role in my imagination in that period, but I was well acquainted with the corrosive effect racial animus had on discourse over American welfare politics. Conducting the research for my PhD dissertation on immigration politics in France and Britain naturally prompted the question whether American-style race relations would be duplicated in Europe. In retrospect, the argument in my essay was perhaps even more recklessly speculative than I recognised at the time.

In the nearly thirty years since publication, 'Migration and the Political Economy of the Welfare State' (hereinafter 'Migration') has been cited according to various indices about 200 times. By my non-exacting standards that is pretty good, but this may be misleading, a rare example of citation counts being inflated due to critical or dismissive references. I have neither time nor stomach to track down the valences of the comments 'Migration' has engendered, but I take the kind invitation of the editors of this volume to revisit this slight essay as an indication that it is possible some parts of the argument still merit discussion, if only to be swatted down.

Looking Back

'Migration' develops a theoretical framework positing that welfare states[2] are inherently closed systems that require boundaries to sort out 'members' from 'non-members'. Welfare states seek to produce economic security and a decent floor of income through the solidaristic logic of mutual trust, a sense of belonging and the experience of common effort and sacrifice. Welfare states attempt to cushion domestic constituencies against the vagaries of national and international free markets. Liberal democratic welfare states operate open economies in a global system marked by the logic of intense competition, extreme inequality and clear winners and losers.

Welfare-state arrangements are meant to mitigate the most common socially 'undesirable' consequences of free markets. They assert the distributive principle of mutual aid according to need against the distributive principle of the market. To that extent welfare states are themselves in contradiction with open economies, and deliberately so. Welfare states raise the cost of doing business through extensive regulations and steep taxes on capital and income. These revenues fund transfer payments that hike the cost of labour by affecting the relative attractiveness of work to leisure. The compatibility of extensive welfare states in the European mould with success in the ruthless global economy of the twenty-first century is the focus of extensive and heated debate. One popular, though to my mind absurd, argument is that mass migration will rescue welfare programmes facing fiscal ruin due to societal ageing. No doubt, a constant influx of young, fertile migrants would feed cash into the social policy accounts and buy time before those programmes crashed. The impossibility of sustaining a flow of the magnitude required to maintain suitable dependency ratios is obvious. Were it possible, the cure for ageing would be worse than the disease. In a very short time the ethnic composition of European societies would by official policy be transformed beyond recognition.

'Migration' did not dwell on the impact of costly welfare states on economic competitiveness and productivity. My focus was on the movement of labour across international borders, especially migration from poorer to richer countries and migration that produced ethnically and culturally mixed societies. A new era of such migration had opened in the rich democracies around 1965, to pick a somewhat arbitrary date. In that year, the USA eliminated the national origins quota system and opened its door to mass immigration over the next sixty years; Canada and Australia followed suit. In Europe, meanwhile, the great guest worker experiments had run off the rails, leading to large-scale and totally unplanned settlement of non-European immigrants, decades of family 'reunification' and formation, followed by mass influxes of refugees and irregular migrants.

By 1985, when I was writing, it was apparent that the liberal democracies were undergoing a social transformation of major proportions with the introduction of racial, ethnic and religious immigrant minorities. The numbers were relatively small, in some countries miniscule, but the dynamic trend was there for anyone to see and it was difficult to imagine a scenario under which the trend would be slowed, let alone reversed.[3] Even if migration could be slowed, differential fertility assured that over a relatively short horizon the immigrant origin population would expand rapidly in comparison to below-replacement fertility among native Europeans.[4]

The empirical claim of 'Migration' was that mass immigration of the sort unfolding in Europe would lead to the erosion of support for the welfare state among native populations and would ratchet up conflict over social benefits and the taxes extracted to pay for them. This would occur (and was occurring) because in the first instance working-class natives would grow to resent what they saw as the exploitation of welfare programmes by undeserving foreigners. Their resentment would be further fuelled as the comfortable middle-class and business, academic, benevolent and political elites, their ramparts at the height of society well insulated, poured contempt on their bigoted and ignorant countrymen. Immigrant labour, meanwhile, would undermine the strategic position of native labour by doing work and accepting wages below European standards and generally by making labour less scarce.

One of the most troubling consequences of mass immigration to European welfare states is that it has engendered the formation of extreme right-wing parties and movements that oppose immigration. In 1986 I was able to point to Enoch Powell, James Schwartzenbach and Jean-Marie Le Pen. Today, writing in the shadow of the Norwegian massacre, I could go on at much greater length about radical right extremist groups. The literature is ample and leaves no doubt as to the connection between immigration and support for the radical right.[5]

What distinguishes immigration-driven conflict over social policy from the run of the mill contentiousness that characterises all discussions of taxation and redistribution of welfare is that it is suffused with racial, ethnic and cultural resentments. It is no longer simply the poor, young louts, layabouts or welfare cheats who are thought to be career spongers taking advantage of benevolent social programmes. It is foreigners. Race has always shaped and deformed the discussion of social policy in the USA. Racial animus is a major explanation for the way the USA lags behind more generous and comprehensive European systems and for the quagmire that discussion of welfare and race often becomes.

American progressives have long anticipated that the USA would finally move beyond these obsessions and develop European-style welfare programmes that appear otherwise to be universal features of advanced societies. My worry was and remains that the introduction of racial and ethnic cleavages in Europe will bring about not the Europeanisation of American welfare politics but instead the Americanisation of European welfare politics.

Critiques

Even some critics concede that arguments like that in my essay enjoy a measure of 'face validity'.[6] I would retort that the argument has a great deal of face validity and it was that ring of truth that has provoked an outpouring of carefully designed and assiduously analysed empirical data purported to poke scientific holes into what critics conceded had become a 'master narrative'.[7] Obviously, when possible, we should go beyond anecdotal impressions to systematic tests against data. At the same time, we must avoid burying the bigger picture that is in plain sight under a blizzard of regression equations and significance tests. The abundant scholarship devoted to uncovering the impact of immigration on the welfare state that has emerged since 1986 has settled a few disputes but has more typically yielded weak statistical relationships and inconclusive results.

One of the most common critiques of the sort of argument advanced in 'Migration' is that it is simply wrong-headed, unjustifiably alarmist and too much influenced by the American experience, which includes African slavery, racial segregation and mass immigration as a settler society, none of which is relevant to Europe. Some Europeans have referred to the argument as the 'American warning';[8] those of us making it have been identified not altogether complimentarily as members of the 'American school'. Our work earns the adjective 'American' because it presumably proceeds from certain 'lessons' of the American experience and because much of the scholarship is produced by Americans or scholars at American institutions.[9]

It was to be expected that any suggestion that Europe was becoming more like the United States would stir up a hornet's nest of indignation and retaliatory responses. These may be valid complaints, but when stated flatly such comments suffer from the very flaws of which I am sometimes accused. They don't amount to a critique so much as the staking out of a position.

Attitudes

One relevant line of empirical inquiry concerns the hierarchy of deservingness Europeans embrace. There is compelling evidence that they distinguish between particular groups in terms of the extent to which they deserve to receive social benefits. Generally, the elderly are ranked most deserving, followed by the sick and disabled, the unemployed, and lastly, immigrants. This finding holds true across countries.[10] A small body of research deals specifically with the relationship between opinion about immigration and opinion about welfare. This literature draws on a variety of data sets and variables, and its results are mixed but weakly consistent with my thesis. Onasch concludes from a major survey of the literature that studies have found a weak negative relationship between support for the welfare state and the perceived presence of immigrants and increasing levels of ethnic diversity.[11] Bay and Pedersen find, on the basis of a national sample of the Norwegian electorate, that a 'persuasion experiment' can mobilise negative attitudes towards immigration and significantly reduce support for a basic income proposal.[12]

A few studies, however, reveal that greater numbers of immigrants are related to more positive attitudes towards redistribution.[13] Van der Waal and his associates find that variations in welfare chauvinism across countries can be accounted for by perceived violations of the norm of reciprocity.[14] The authors argue that neither ethnic diversity nor ethnic competition theories are necessary to explain cross-national variation once left-party participation in government is taken into account.[15]

Social capital or generalised trust have been identified as a mechanism for bridging group differences and are thought to be a basic ingredient of stable and prosperous democracies.[16] When a comparative study found that diversity and trust were negatively related, extraordinary steps were taken to soften the normative implications.[17] Crepaz has produced the most extensive comparative exposition of the effects of migration and diversity on generalised social trust.[18] He finds that trust is relatively resistant to erosion by immigration and diversity, because institutions and policies can reduce their negative consequences.

Path Dependency and Historical Sequences

One of the most telling criticisms of the 'American warning' has to do with timing, or path dependence. As Banting has pointed out, the sequencing of diversity and welfare is remarkably different in Europe and America. In the latter, slavery and migration from Europe, China and South America preceded the establishment of even rudimentary welfare provisions by at least two centuries.[19] Hence, racial, religious and linguistic cleavages were well established before proposals for state-supported social protection schemes were touted. As such, they constituted an effective deterrent to consensus on sharing risk across social groups.

Europe, on the other hand, had built the most comprehensive welfare systems in the world before immigrant-based diversity emerged as a concern in the 1950s. Moreover, social democratic parties and affiliated trade unions, the main architects of the welfare state, had organised and assumed power as diversity developed. An existing and strongly supported welfare state enjoyed a position, therefore, from which to weather the storms of ethnic conflict and to reduce its emergence in the first place. Variations in timing and sequencing mean that we should anticipate different forms of ethnic/welfare-state conflict across nations. In America, racial and ethnic conflict has not only slowed the introduction of social programmes but has been a cause of their selective and contributory form as well as their modest generosity.

Geddes raises another timing issue, noting that immigration is not the main factor pushing welfare state programmes to reform.[20] Rather, changes in the global economy are the main factor. Immigration is not driving welfare reform. Welfare-state pressures emanating from the external economy are driving immigration by creating dislocations in both sending and receiving societies.

Immigration and Welfare Policy

Among the most ambitious critiques of the 'American warning' are those rooted in comparative analyses designed to test the thesis against dependent variables that measure welfare policy rather than public attitudes. That significant variation exists is taken both as evidence that the American model is misbegotten and as an invitation to investigate the factors that account for the various outcomes.[21] These are often grouped under three headings: different welfare regimes, different types of migration and different types of diversity. There is a tripartite typology of welfare regimes: liberal, corporatist and social democratic.

From this perspective, the 'welfare state' doesn't exist as a universal construct.[22] Migration, itself, can be disaggregated into numerous categories: legal/illegal, skilled/unskilled, permanent/temporary, economic/refugee and wanted/unwanted. Finally, diversity comes in many forms: race, ethnicity, religion and language.

Honing in on the measurement of the dependent and independent variables produces results that are in some cases consistent with my thesis and in others not. For example, social democratic and corporatist welfare regimes are seen to be less vulnerable or open to ethnic conflict over immigration than are the liberal regimes most similar to the USA.[23] Among types of migrants, asylum seekers are more often the target of complaints about welfare use than legal skilled workers. And not all diversity provokes the sorts of animosities that others do. Although highly skilled migrants from within the EU sometimes provoke opposition, they are generally more readily accommodated than Muslim migrants from the European periphery.

A large and consistent body of research on the impact of race on American attitudes toward welfare and on the quality and generosity of American social programmes at federal and state level demonstrates a linkage between racial or ethnic fragmentation and actual spending on welfare programmes.[24] This research largely supports the claim that more diverse societies and communities tend to support less generous welfare programmes. Evidence also suggests that more heterogeneous societies display lower levels of support for redistributive welfare programmes, exhibit lower levels of social trust, and spend less, on average, for social welfare and redistributive programmes than more homogeneous societies.[25]

According to Banting, history shows that diversity and immigration are not always detrimental to the welfare state. Not all multiculturalism is based on immigration; there is also sub-state nationalism. The Scandinavian countries were homogeneous before immigration changed things. Another set of countries was deeply divided but with consociational institutions. A final group (the United States, Canada and Switzerland) was diverse but lacked those institutions: There is *prima facie* evidence from the postwar era, he argues, that linguistic/ethnic diversity does constrain social welfare redistribution. However, the relationship is highly contingent and mediated by political institutions. Bommes and Geddes conclude that welfare states have introduced diversified categories of migrants linked with different clusters of rights and restrictions.[26] This can be seen as an effort to reaffirm external closure and as the basis for internal inclusion. The perspective that 'migration is a threat to welfare' is much too abstract and general. Migrants are perceived and are treated differently depending on the internal infrastructure of welfare states, different traditions of immigration, diverse legal traditions and other factors. They suggest that research should zero in 'on national settings, national political institutional repertoires that structure migration regimes, and on the immigration and immigrant policies that all pave the path to social participation'.

Sanderson hypothesises that 'Ethnically heterogeneous societies should have less public spending because people are more reluctant to incur costs to provide for others when those others are much less likely to belong to their own ethnic group'.[27] Analysing data for 121 countries and employing several different measures of ethnic heterogeneity, he finds 'ethnic heterogeneity is a very important predictor of a society's level of welfare spending'.[28]

Soroka, Banting and Johnston is a rare study of the impact of immigration itself (as opposed to ethnic fragmentation) on welfare spending.[29] They show that although no welfare-state has actually shrunk in the face of the accelerating immigration in recent years, the rate of growth of spending is significantly smaller the more open a society is to immigration. Flows of foreigners are negatively related to spending on welfare-state programmes. The typical industrial society, they estimate, might spend 16–17 per cent more than it now does on social services if it had kept its foreign-born percentage where it was in 1970!

The economist Alberto Alesina and his associates compare the effect of diversity on welfare regimes in the USA and Europe.[30] Alesina, Glaeser and Sacerdote show that Europeans and Americans differ sharply in their opinions about the poor.[31] Europeans typically view the poor as unfortunate but not personally responsible, while in the USA there is less sympathy and an assumption of personal responsibility. They find that the more people there are who believe that income differences across individuals are driven by luck, the larger is the share of social spending.[32] Additionally, the greater the share of the poor composed of racial or ethnic minorities, the lower are expenditures on social programmes. They conclude: 'Racial fragmentation in the United States and the disproportionate representation of ethnic minorities among the poor clearly played a major role in limiting redistribution, and indeed, racial cleavages seem to serve as a barrier to redistribution throughout the world.'[33]

Alesina and Glaeser argue that about half the gap in welfare spending between the USA and Europe is explained by institutional factors (majoritarianism, federalism, separation of powers), but that racial heterogeneity explains the bulk of the other half of the differences either directly, whatever the political institutions, or indirectly through institutional variables.[34] Countries that are more racially fragmented spend less on welfare than more homogeneous countries. These findings have been contested by Taylor-Gooby.[35] His critique is built in part on the historical sequences of developments discussed above. To wit, he notes that Alesina and Glaeser use standard OECD measures of social spending as a percentage of GDP as the dependent variable and measures of ethno-linguistic and racial fractionalisation as the independent variable. The former is not significant, whereas the latter is highly significant. Their model covers 56 countries. Taylor-Gooby redoes the analysis for just 21 advanced democracies and inserts measures of left party presence. He finds 'diversity does have a negative impact on welfare spending, but one that is much weaker and less significant in the advanced welfare states outside the US'. His data also show that for the 21 countries outside the USA the correlation between diversity and spending is much reduced taking the impact of left politics into account.[36]

Conclusion

Looking back at something written three decades ago is both a welcome opportunity and an exercise filled with peril. If nothing seems to have turned out as expected, there is no honest way to hide that fact. On the other hand, if you admit no mistakes, you risk appearing blind to alternative arguments. Nevertheless, few of the predictions I mooted have been proven false. Of those subjected to empirical test, only a handful have rendered definitive results, and the bolder predictions I chanced, involving as they do dynamic processes, are not easily put to an empirical test with snapshot data taken from national sample surveys.

How the mass immigration that is transforming European societies will affect their political economies is still an open question. Two observers can draw quite different conclusions from the same developments. My view is that theory suggests that ethnically diverse societies tend to be marked by conflict and low levels of trust. What we know about the history of ethnically divided societies leads me to a similar conclusion.

Disaggregation of multidimensional concepts is normally a good thing. I have argued for just that approach for understanding the political decision-making process as it unfolds with respect to different aspects of immigration politics in different countries.[37] The danger is that in whittling down generalisations into less comprehensive and more narrowly construed hypotheses we will be, again, led away from the more important broad contours of our subject. In an effort to avoid making statements that are too inclusive, we risk being consigned to dealing with trivia. Take for example the observation that European regimes are engaged in a dramatic exercise in walking away from multicultural policies that are now deeply regretted. It is likely to be countered by claims that no such pattern exists because this country is still committed to multiculturalism, while that country is only temporarily trying something new, and other countries are responding to political pressure from the radical right rather than backtracking out of legitimate concerns. All the more specific statements may be accurate, but in focusing on them we may overlook the broader drift of policy.

How well do the arguments in 'Migration' hold up thirty years hence? Or, as Chou En-lai famously answered when asked to offer a verdict on the French revolution, is it too soon to tell? More often than not, events in the last three decades seem roughly consistent with my argument. Nothing that transpired since 1986 caused me to slap myself upside the head and think that I was wrong and that the rapid ethnic transformation of European societies has, against the dismal experience of all human history, caused hardly a ripple. Of course, welfare states that had been constructed over more than a century were not dismantled over night; pensioners did not march in the streets demanding an end to the subsidisation of their retirement; immigrants in Europe were not systematically excluded from benefits rolls. But the tenor of debate over social benefits certainly changed for the worse and complaints about foreign scroungers became common fare on the political right. Without channelling Chou En-lai, I might caution those who have declared victory for multicultural societies in Europe that all the evidence is far from in.

I am inclined to stand by the article in its broadest terms. I believed then and am even more convinced today that there is a contradiction between open borders and comprehensive welfare states. To put it more directly, the 'universal' norms and values proclaimed by the European community – equality, freedom, tolerance, democracy, common citizenship, secularism, the resolution of conflicts through negotiation and support for a comprehensive welfare state – are incompatible with the mass immigration, free movement and divided multicultural societies that necessarily follow. Idealistic progressives who believe they can have both are, in my opinion, victims of a delusion.

Notes

1. Freeman, G. 'Migration and the Political Economy of the Welfare State'. *The Annals of the American Academy of Political and Social Science*, 485 (1986): 51–63.

2. I mean specifically the various programmes common to all liberal democracies designed to mitigate economic risk and inequality and more generally the mixed political economies common in the postwar West.

3. Caldwell, C. *Reflections on the Revolution in Europe: Immigration, Islam, and the West.* New York: Doubleday, 2009.

4. Kaufmann, E. *Shall the Religious Inherit the Earth? Demography and Politics in the Twenty-First Century.* Profile Books: London, 2010.

5. Messina, A. *The Logics and Politics of Post-WWII Migration to Western Europe.* New York: Cambridge University Press, 2007, pp. 54–96; Mudde, C. *Populist Radical Right Parties in Europe.* New York: Cambridge University Press, 2007; Betz, H-G. *Radical Right-wing Populism in Western Europe.* New York: St. Martin's Press, 1994; Givens, T. *Voting Radical Right in Western Europe.* Cambridge: Cambridge University Press, 2005; Art, D. *Inside the Radical Right: The Development of Anti-Immigrant Parties in Western Europe.* New York: Cambridge University Press, 2011.

6. Van der Waal, J., Achterberg, P. and van Oorschot, W. 'Why Are in Some European Countries Immigrants Considered less Entitled to Welfare?' Presented at the NORFACE Conference, London, April 2011, p. 3.

7. Kymlicka, W. and Banting, K. 'Immigration, Multiculturalism, and the Welfare State'. *Ethics & International Affairs*, 20/3 (2006): 286.

8. Van Oorschot: 'Making the Difference in Social Europe: Deservingness Perceptions among Citizens of European Welfare States'. *Journal of European Social Policy*, 161 (2006): 23–42.

9. A more accurate label would be the US school, as Canadian scholars have been at the forefront contesting the diversity thesis. See Kymlicka and Banting: 'Immigration, Multiculturalism, and the Welfare State', pp. 281–304.

10. Van Oorschot: 'Making the Difference in Social Europe'; Van Oorschot, W. 'Solidarity towards Immigrants in European Welfare States'. *International Journal of Social Welfare*, 17/1 (2008): 3–14.

11. Onasch, E. 'Racial Diversity and Welfare in Europe: Tracing the Formation and Consequences of Racialized National Identities'. Presented for NordWel/REASSESS Summer School, Odense, August 2010: 15–20; Senik, C., Stichnoth, H. and Van der

Straeten, K. 'Immigration and Natives' Attitudes Towards the Welfare State: Evidence from the European Social Survey'. *Social Indicators Research*, 91/3 (2009): 345–70; Coenders, M. and Scheepers, P. 'Changes in Resistance to the Social Integration of Foreigners in Germany 1980–2000: Individual and Contextual Determinants'. *Journal of Ethnic & Migration Studies*, 34 (2008): 11.

12. Bay, A-H. and Pedersen, A. 'The Limits of Social Solidarity: Basic Income, Immigration and the Legitimacy of the Universal Welfare State'. *Acta Sociologica*, 49/4 (2006): 419–36.

13. Sundberg, T. 'Immigration and Attitudes to Welfare: Ethnic Fractionalisation is not the Culprit for Negative Welfare Attitudes'. Unpublished manuscript; Van Oorschot, W. and Uunk, W. 'Welfare Spending and the Public's Concern for Immigrants: Multilevel Evidence for Eighteen European Countries'. *Comparative Politics*, 40/1 (2007): 63–82.

14. Van der Waal et al.: 'Why Are in Some European Countries Immigrants Considered less Entitled to Welfare?'

15. See also Goul Andersen, J. 'Immigration and the Legitimacy of the Scandinavian Welfare State: Some Preliminary Danish Findings'. AMID Working Paper Series, 53/2006.

16. Putnam, R. *Bowling Alone: The Collapse and Revival of American Community*. New York: Simon & Schuster, 2000.

17. Putnam, R. 'E Pluribus Unum: Diversity and Community in the Twenty-first Century – The 2006 Johan Skytte Prize Lecture'. *Scandinavian Political Studies*, 30/2 (2007): 137–74.

18. Crepaz, M. *Trust Beyond Borders: Immigration, the Welfare State, and Identity in Modern Societies*. Ann Arbor: University of Michigan Press, 2008.

19. Banting, K. 'Looking in Three Directions: Migration and the European Welfare State in Comparative Perspective'. In M. Bommes and A. Geddes (eds) *Immigration and Welfare: Challenging the Borders of the Welfare State*. London: Routledge, 2000.

20. Geddes, A. 'Migration and the Welfare State in Europe'. *The Political Quarterly*, 74/51 (2003): 150–62.

21. Banting: 'Looking in Three Directions'.

22. Esping-Andersen, G. *The Three Worlds of Welfare Capitalism*. New York: Polity Press, 1990.

23. Larsen, C. 'The Institutional Logic of Welfare Attitudes: How Welfare Regimes Influence Public Support'. *Comparative Political Studies*, 41 (2008): 145–69.

24. Alesina, A., Baqir, R. and Easterly, W. 'Public Goods and Ethnic Divisions'. *Quarterly Journal of Economics*, 114 (November 1999): 1243–84; Hero, R. and Tolbert, C. 'A Racial/Ethnic Diversity Interpretation of Politics and Policy in the States of the US'. *American Journal of Political Science*, 40 (1996): 851–71; Plotnick, R. and Winters, R. 'A Politico-Economic Theory of Income Redistribution'. *American Political Science Review*, 79 (1985): 458–73; Brown, R. 'Party Cleavages and Welfare Effort in the American States'. *American Political Science Review*, 89 (1995): 29–33; Radcliff, B. and Saiz, M. 'Race, Turnout, and Public Policy in the American States'. Paper presented at the Annual Meeting of the Western Political Science Association, Albuquerque, 1994; Fellowes, M. and Rowe, G. 'Politics and the New American Welfare State'. *American Journal of Political Science*, 48 (April 2004): 362–73; Soss, J., et al. 'Setting the Terms of Relief: Explaining State Policy Choices in the Devolution Revolution'. *American Journal of Political Science*, 45/2 (2001): 378–95; and Hero, R. and Preuhs, R. 'Immigration and the Evolving American Welfare State: Examining Policies in the U.S. States'. *American Journal of Political Science*, 51 (2007): 498–517.

25. Alesina, A. and La Ferrara, E. 'Who Trusts Others?'. *Journal of Public Economics*, 85 (2002): 207–34; Luttmer, E. 'Group Loyalty and the Taste for Redistribution'. *Journal of Political Economy*, 109/3 (2001): 500–28.

26. Bommes, M. and Geddes, A. 'Conclusion'. In M. Bommes. and A. Geddes (eds) *Immigration and Welfare: Challenging the Borders of the Welfare State*. London: Routledge, 2000, p. 245.

27. Sanderson, S. 'Ethnic Heterogeneity and Public Spending: Testing the Evolutionary Theory of Ethnicity with Cross-national Data'. In F. Salter (ed.) *Welfare, Ethnicity, and Altruism: New Findings and Evolutionary Theory*. London: Frank Cass, 2004, p. 74.

28. Cf. Vanhanen, T. 'An Exploratory Comparative Study of the Relationship between Ethnic Heterogeneity and Welfare Politics'. InF. Salter (ed.) *Welfare, Ethnicity, and Altruism*. London: Frank Cass, 2004; Sanderson, S. and Vanhanen, T. 'Reconciling the Differences between Sanderson's and Vanhanen's Results'. In F. Salter (ed.) *Welfare, Ethnicity, and Altruism*. London: Frank Cass, 2004.

29. Soroka, S., Banting, K. and Johnston, R. 'Immigration and Redistribution in a Global Era'. In P. Bardhan, S. Bowles and M. Wallerstein (eds) *Globalization and Egalitarian Redistribution*. New York: Russell Sage Foundation, 2006.

30. Alesina et al.: 'Public Goods and Ethnic Divisions', pp. 1243–84; Alesina and La Ferrara: 'Who Trusts Others?', pp. 207–34.

31. Alesina, A., Glaeser, E. and Sacerdote, B. 'Why Doesn't the United States have a European-style Welfare State?'. *Brookings Papers on Economic Activity* (Fall 2001): 187–248.

32. Alesina et al.: 'Why Doesn't the United States have a European-style Welfare State?', p. 238.

33. Alesina et al.: 'Why Doesn't the United States have a European-style Welfare State?', p. 248.

34. Alesina, A. and Glaeser, E. *Fighting Poverty in the US and Europe: A World of Difference*. Oxford: Oxford University Press, 2004, p. 133.

35. Taylor-Gooby, P. 'Is the Future American? Or, Can Left Politics Preserve European Welfare States from Erosion through Growing "Racial" Diversity?' *Journal of Social Policy*, 34/04 (2005): 661–72.

36. So far as I can tell, Alesina and associates have not responded to Taylor-Gooby's criticisms. They are, however, frequently cited as definitive refutations of their work.

37. Freeman, G. 'National Models, Policy Types, and the Politics of Immigration'. In V. Guiraudon and G. Lahav (eds) *Immigration Policy in Europe: The Politics of Control.* New York: Routledge, 2007.

Further Reading

Freeman, G., Hansen, R. and Leal, D. (eds) *Immigration and Public Opinion in Liberal Democracies.* New York: Routledge, 2012.

CHAPTER 2

European Movements of Labour: Challenges for European Social Models[1]

Jon Erik Dølvik

Introduction

European debates about migration and the welfare state have most commonly centred on immigration from outside Europe, and the ways in which best to enable labour-market integration and prevent welfare dependency among the growing populations of refugees, asylum-seekers and their families. Migration within the European Community was – after the ebbing of the post-war flows of Italian migrants – relatively modest and attracted little attention. As well as reflecting the discouraging influence of cultural and linguistic differences, the low rate of mobility pointed to the relative homogeneity of wages and living conditions within the 'old' member states. The lifting of the Iron Curtain marked a historical turning point also in this respect, initiating a period during which rising labour migration in Europe culminated with the eastern enlargements of the EU and EEA in 2004 and 2007. The gap in wages and welfare within one common labour market was unprecedented. While living standards in the southern accession countries in the 1980s were around 65 per cent of the EC average, living standards in the eastern accession states were on average 45 per cent of those in EU15, the countries of Western Europe which made up the European Union prior to the accession in 2004. Nominal wages in the eastern accession states ranged from one-tenth to one-seventh of those in EU15.[2] In spite of the transitional restrictions established for free movement of labour in many countries, this unleashed the largest intra-European movement of labour in modern times. After the Baltic states had seen up to 10 per cent of their populations emigrating during the 1990s, the number of New Member

State (NMS) residents in the EU15 increased from around 2 million in 2004 to almost 5 million in 2009.[3] Additional to this were the many posted and self-employed workers who also moved west, implying that the gross flows were much larger. In many countries these flows by far exceeded the streams of migrants arriving from outside the EU through the 'humanitarian gate'.[4]

Besides the huge gap in wages and welfare – comparable to that between Mexico and USA – the flows were fuelled by the economic bonanza in the West and surpluses of labour in the NMS.[5] Thus, in the main sending country, Poland, the number of people working abroad more than doubled in three years – from 1 million to 2.3 million – while domestic unemployment fell from 19 per cent to 7 per cent.[6] And when Europe went into recession after the financial crunch in 2008, the total flow of immigration declined. Outflows from crisis-stricken countries, such as the Baltic states and Romania, continued to rise, however, and the number of citizens from NMS working in the West continued to grow. At the same time the rise in unemployment and the fall in employment rates were much stronger among NMS migrants than in the native populations.[7] When the debt crisis and mass unemployment hit Ireland and the southern flank of the EU, jobseekers from these countries added to the flows.

Seen from this angle, it becomes obvious that the impact of migration on labour markets and welfare states in Europe cannot be discussed without taking into account, first, the rise in intra-EU migration and its implications for immigrants from countries out-side the EU, and, second, the endogenous changes in national labour markets and welfare states that evolved during the past decades of market and monetary integration, culminating in the euro-crisis and the sweeping changes in economic governance and social policies that followed. Hence, viable national strategies to link immigration, labour-market and welfare policies can hardly be developed without taking into account the interaction between migration flows within and external to the EU, and the ramifications provided by the multi-level EU regime in this context. It is worth noting that a presumption underlying this regime is that labour migrants from the EU/EEA ought to have priority when hiring foreign labour.

In this chapter, we briefly discuss how the rise in intra-EU labour migration may influence the challenges facing European welfare states and labour-market regimes (social models). Whilst the growth in intra-EU mobility after enlargement has generally been viewed as triple-win process benefiting the migrants as well as both the sending and receiving states,[8] a more detailed analysis reveals a picture that is decidedly more ambiguous. This chapter will focus on the labour markets of the receiving states, where the effects of greater inflows of labour on equality, wages and employment conditions in low-end occupations have spurred controversy and demands for re-regulation.[9] The implications for labour-market participation among immigrants from non-European countries and other vulnerable groups have also spurred debate about whether the new labour migration will serve as a rescue or a threat for the ailing European welfare states.[10] Furthermore, important questions have been raised about the effects of the high outflow of educated labour for the social models in the NMS, where populations are ageing at a stronger rate than in the West.[11]

The first section will sketch the background and regulatory context of labour migration within the EU/European Free Trade Association (EFTA) area. A rough overview of the magnitude and pattern of such migration since 2004 will then be provided. The final section will discuss the challenges entailed in facilitating sustainable labour migration and the responses of social actors and governments in receiving member states, and suggest that re-regulation of the European labour markets is key to enhancing sound labour migration and rescuing European social models.

Development and Regulation of Labour Migration in the EU

The essential purpose of national industrial relations systems is to ensure equal treatment for equal work by creating a floor of wages and working conditions that take wages out of competition between firms in the same industry.[12] The welfare state has in most countries underpinned this purpose by providing a 'reservation wage' that bolsters workers' bargaining power with employers. But when the markets for labour and services are widened, either by extension of their outer boundaries or by the abolition of barriers to labour migration, national wage floors can become subject to erosion, and the effective coverage of collective agreements will tend to shrink because migrant labour and foreign companies are usually difficult to organise. Competition for jobs and job-related rights to social security can also make it tempting for migrant labourers to accept wages below the going rate. For such reasons, and to ensure a level playing field for workers and companies of different nationalities, the EC from early on stipulated that labour migrants taking advantage of the right to free movement should be secured equal treatment in the labour market and social security systems of the host countries.[13] With only modest migration, the dual track of European integration – whereby economic and market integration was governed by supranational EU law, and labour and social issues were governed by the member states – worked smoothly for many decades.

In the early 1990s, with greater European integration on the cards, perceptions began to change. The relaunch of the four freedoms enshrined in the 1992 project, the Maastricht programme of monetary integration, German reunification, and the rising influx of cheap foreign labour into building sites in Berlin, Paris and Brussels, all meant that the question of wage competition in the labour market became more salient. While discussions ran high about the risk of 'regime competition' and 'social dumping' in the European single market, the notion of 'semi-sovereign welfare states' suggested that the member states – due to the EU regime for social security coordination related to labour migration – had lost control over which and how many people would be entitled to social benefits.[14] The 'social dimension' of the single market, launched in the mid-1980s, was meant to curb such problems, and during the 1990s, the Maastricht Social Protocol enabled the adoption of a range of minimum directives concerning worker rights – sometimes resulting from framework agreements negotiated by the social partners. The issue of pay and collective action had been kept outside the EU legislative mandate, however, leaving the member states to ensure that their respective national pay floors and collective bargaining systems were kept intact under the free flow regime of the single market.

In response to the influx of foreign construction and hiring companies employing labour on terms and conditions way below national standards, first France (1993), then Austria (1993) and at last Germany (1995) adopted national legislation concerning wages and working conditions for workers posted from abroad, building on old schemes for extension of collective agreements.[15] This paved the way for adoption of the EU Posting of Workers Directive in 1996, the purpose of which was to strike a balance between securing the access of service providers of all member states to national markets and securing proper conditions for posted workers and fair competition for host country workers.[16] The Directive stipulated that host countries should require foreign service-providers to comply with a core list of working conditions, including minimum wages, laid down in statute or in extended collective agreements.[17] In the decision of the Court of Justice of the European Union (CJEU) in the 'Laval Quartet' of 2007,[18] it was made clear that this list of conditions was considered exhaustive and that only minimum conditions could be applied.

After the Accession Agreement paved the way for the eastward enlargement in 2004 and 2007, all the 'old' member states, except the UK, Ireland and Sweden, reneged on their promise of free movement of workers from day one. Due to domestic concerns about vast influx of Eastern labour and 'welfare scroungers', transitional arrangements were enacted to curb the free movement of workers from the NMS for a maximum of 5 + 2 years. Varying in strictness and conditions, these arrangements certainly influenced the pattern and direction of labour migration but did not stem the flow.[19] Except for Bulgaria and Romania, the last restrictions were repealed on 1 May 2011. As no such restrictions applied to workers posted from foreign companies, except in Germany and Austria, the result was that much labour migration was re-directed into the channel of cross-border services, including leasing of labour through temporary work agencies, sub-contracting and self-employment.[20]

With the unprecedented influx of labour migration seen in many countries, the problem of creating, maintaining and enforcing effective wage floors and mandatory working conditions became a topic of contested industrial relations debate within the western EU and EFTA states. This was accentuated by prior transformations of the national labour markets and social benefits systems. Partial deregulation, company restructuring, trade union decline, the weakening of collective agreements and the rise in flexible employment since the 1990s had in many countries resulted in growing labour-market dualisation associated with rising low-paid, atypical and sometimes precarious work.[21] In the NMS the fragmentation of labour markets has been more profound.[22] Recently, aggravated by the recession and debt crisis in the wake of the financial crunch, this has made the unions' task of maintaining an effective wage floor, especially in low-skilled occupations, both more urgent and more difficult. During the crisis, cuts in welfare-state benefits have compounded the problem.

After reviewing the trends in labour migration in the next section, we will return to their consequences and the respective responses of member states and their social partners.

Post-2004 Developments in Posting and Labour Migration

The opening of EU/EFTA labour markets to the east from 2004 was a bold move. Nowhere before had politicians agreed to allow the free movement of services and labour within an area with more than 500 million inhabitants and wages and welfare gaps of such magnitude. Due to the transitional arrangements providing temporary restrictions on the free movement of workers,[23] and more lenient rules on labour rights, wage setting, taxation and social security contributions for workers posted by foreign companies, the use of service providers from the NMS became an attractive recruitment option for Western companies.[24]

What the Figures Reveal About the Free Movement of Workers in Europe

Labour mobility from the NMS grew rapidly. In the main sending countries, such as Poland, Romania and the Baltic states,

4–10 per cent of the population, corresponding to 6–14 per cent of the labour force, had moved abroad to work by 2009.[25] While during the period 1990–2003, on average, 215,000 EU8 workers had entered EU15 annually, an average of 650,000 yearly entries were registered in the period 2004–7, hitting a record high of 708,000 in 2007.[26] Poland and Romania, as the biggest countries, accounted for three quarter of the outflows, while the UK, Germany and Ireland were the largest receivers of Polish and Baltic migrants, whereas Spain and Italy were the largest receivers of migrants from Romania and Bulgaria. The UK had by 2008 registered more than 800,000 new labour migrants from the new eastern member states, 300,000–400,000 had moved to Ireland, several hundred thousand to Germany, and some 225,000 to Nordic countries,[27] while continental countries, such as the Netherlands, Belgium and France, also received sizeable flows of registered workers. In addition to the stock of almost 5 million migrants from the NMS residing in the EU15 by 2009 came sizeable flows of temporary labour migrants, posted workers, self-employed service providers and unregistered labour.[28] The volume of the movement of labour was much higher than officially expected.[29] Brücker et al. (2009) estimated that the number of NMS citizens residing in EU15 by 2020 would reach 8.4 million, but the current crisis in Southern Europe is likely to slow inflows.[30]

For labour migrants, enlargement brought new opportunities to improve their earnings, skills and career prospects, and to explore the world. The sending countries were relieved of surplus labour and received increased remittances. For companies from both the sending and receiving countries it opened new business opportunities, and for receiving countries the extra supply of labour contributed to higher growth and lower inflation. Adverse effects in the labour markets were negligible according to most studies, although some substitution effects and reduced wage growth were reported in occupations with high inflows and low skill requirements in particular.[31] To Brussels, this seemed a veritable win–win process for all. Most of the flows were considered demand-driven, short-term and circular.

The labour migrants from the NMS countries were younger and better educated than was the workforce in the sending countries. Yet a majority was employed in low-skilled, low-paid jobs, indicating considerable skill mismatches and 'brain-waste'.[32] At the same time, indications of growing skill shortages were reported in main sending countries, and the World Bank warned against severe drain of human resources in the ageing NMS.[33] During the 2008–9 crisis, the total outflow of labour migrants from East European states declined, but the predicted rise in return migration never really materialised, and the severe economic fallout in sending countries, such as the Baltic states and Romania, engendered sustained outflows. Hence, from 2008 to 2010, the number of employed citizens from the NMS increased in all but two of the 15 pre-2004 member states – Spain and Ireland – in spite of rising unemployment rates among NMS residents in most EU15 countries.[34]

Such figures question the view that the new, freer flow of migration between Eastern and Western Europe is predominantly temporary and circular in nature. According to this common view, the existing patterns of migration serve simply to enhance skill formation and flexibility of labour supply in the home states, and to resolve temporary bottlenecks in the host countries. In the case of Poland, for example, though the outflow of temporary labour migrants declined substantially after the financial crisis, the proportion of those remaining abroad for longer periods has increased markedly since 2009, and the number that settles is reported to be growing.[35] In the Baltic states, estimates suggest that as much as 10 per cent of the remaining population has left since the economic collapse in 2008.[36] Taking into account the fact that a significant share of those leaving are young and well educated – and that those who return tend to be less skilled than the emigrant cohorts from which they came – this exit of 15–20 per cent of the labour force represents a major drain on already scarce human resources.[37] During the subsequent early recovery, this has led to acute shortages of skilled labour, not least in the health and medical sector, prompting government campaigns to entice 'young talents' to return home, which have so far met with only limited success.[38] In Norway, which relative to population has been one of largest recipients of labour from the Baltic states and Poland, inflows have continued to rise.[39] In a survey among Polish labour migrants in Oslo 2010, almost

40 per cent of the interviewees were out of work – 14 per cent were registered unemployed – but only a small minority of those had concrete plans of returning home.[40] Among those in work, less than one fifth had a permanent job. Increased settlement among labour migrants from the NMS and their families has in recent years contributed to all time high net immigration – of which a net rise of about 10,000 Baltic and 10,000 Polish citizens in 2011.[41]

Posting of Workers

While workers moving under the auspices of free movement of labour are entitled to equal treatment by their host country employers, the rights that apply to workers posted by foreign subcontractors and temp agencies, or operating as self-employed, are much more limited. The increased access to posted labour has therefore engendered a shift in employment practices that poses pressures on labour market institutions of the host country. This was accentuated by the CJEU decisions in the 'Laval Quartet', a series of cases concerning the rules that the host states can apply to posted workers. The court's ruling restricted the rights of such workers to a statutory minimum and declared host country's collective action aimed at securing posted workers' conditions beyond this minimum to be unlawful. As a consequence, the EU has faced a trilemma of fundamental rights between the freedom to provide services, the right of workers to non-discrimination and equal treatment, and the right to collective action.[42] While all these rights are enshrined in the EU Treaty, and the latter two are also in the Charter and in UN conventions, the Commission attempt to resolve the quandary by the proposed Monti-II regulation met with strong protests from governments and unions alike, and the proposal was subsequently withdrawn.[43] The proposed formula for reconciling free movement and the right to collective action remains, it seems, well within the straightjacket defined by the CJEU in Laval.

Because registration schemes for posted workers are deemed 'disproportionate restrictions' on the freedom to provide services, no viable European statistics for their numbers exist. Referring to the numbers of issued E101 social insurance formulas that people working abroad 'shall carry with them', the Commission has asserted that the flows of posted workers have been modest.[44] According to a recent study, roughly 1 million E101 certificates were issued to posted workers in 2007, accounting for 0.4 per cent of the labour force in EU15.[45] The number of certificates rose by 24 per cent in 2005–7, while the figures stagnated during the crisis of 2008–9. Experience in countries with compulsory registration for posted workers, however, suggests that the Commission figures vastly underestimate the actual flows of posted workers. In Belgium, 99,000 E101 certificates were registered in 2007, whereas the national database on notification of posted workers indicates that the number was substantially higher – 145,000 in 2007 and more than 200,000 in 2008.[46] In Switzerland the registered number of posted workers increased from 93,000 in 2005 to 127,000 in 2009, which constituted 41 per cent of all migrant labour while self-employed constituted an additional 11 per cent. In Norway, where EU workers account for roughly 10 per cent of the labour force, analyses of tax registry data indicate that posted workers accounted for almost half of the gross labour inflows in the years 2004–8.[47]

If we look at the sectors where posting is most common, case studies in European shipyards suggest that around 50 per cent of the workforce is comprised of labour from the NMS, but hired by foreign subcontractors and temp agencies. Some of the posted workers eventually become recruited by the yards, but they only constitute a minor share of the in-house workforce.[48] In construction, studies estimate that workers posted to host countries by their employers account for 10–15 per cent of employment in Germany, Britain and Denmark, and around 20 per cent in Finland.[49] In the Netherlands and Germany a strong rise was seen particularly in self-employed contractors. Whatever the exact numbers are, these figures indicate that postings of workers account for a sizeable share of intra-EU/EFTA labour migration, and have contributed to changes in the hiring practices of companies that make it more difficult for the host states and unions to ensure proper conditions.

The dynamics behind the growth of cross-border subcontracting are complex. First, most countries have over the past 15 years seen

a general restructuring trend towards more project-based organisations, outsourcing and contract flexibility, leading to increased segmentation and sharper divisions between the labour market core and
periphery.[50] Second, the East–West gap in labour costs pertaining to
pay, taxes, employer levies and social charges – likely to be complemented by a growing South–North gap in the wake of the debt crisis – is
a major economic incentive for clients, contractors and posted workers. Splitting the difference among them may be irresistible, and with
the logistical infrastructure provided by websites, cheap air-carriers
and migratory networks a mushrooming flora of agents, middlemen
and hiring-firms has grown.

Dualisation, Regime Shopping and the Blurring of Boundaries

While the general figures show that the rise in labour migration has
benefited the majority of workers and sectors, these trends have reinforced domestic developments towards more fluid and flexible employment practices in the lower ends of the labour market and have
blurred the boundaries between different categories of migrant labour.
For a Polish worker going to London, Berlin or Oslo, it is not uncom-
mon to shift between temporary jobs in a firm established in the host
country, spells of self-employment, and short-term assignments for
foreign sub-contractors and temp agencies, intermittent with periods
of joblessness.[51] As these statuses, according to EU law, are subject to
different social and labour rights, companies have been enabled to develop new forms of 'regime shopping' and circumvention in order to
increase flexibility and lower labour costs. The likely result is growing
downward differentiation in the labour market.

During the crisis, foreign workers employed by sub-contractors
and temp agencies were usually the first to face redundancy, serving
as an external cushion for the core workers.[52] Under the slow recovery in 2009 and 2010, as much as 85 per cent of net employment
growth in the EU came in the form of temporary jobs. Though this
share may have fallen somewhat since 2011, the interaction between
higher unemployment in the wake of crisis and austerity, national

labour market dualisation and increased cross-border mobility are likely to reinforce job competition in the second tiers of European labour markets and make it harder for vulnerable groups to gain access. Brenke et al. (2010), studying free movement of workers, thus found that EU8 migrants in Germany more often compete with immigrants from outside Europe than with native workers.[53] The increased reliance which many companies place on temporary external labour also tends to reduce the effective reach of national industrial relations institutions.

In addition to media stories about the unequal treatment, underpayment and abuse of foreign workers, the turn to sub-contracting, leasing and other forms of external labour has been subject to disputes and social tensions. Disputes at Irish Ferries, Gama, Laval, Viking, Lindsay, Tönnies and Pocheville may have made their way into the news headlines, but under the radar working life seems to be changing in ways that make it more difficult for politicians and organised actors to influence and improve.

The mixed picture of continued migratory outflows from NMS, alongside rising unemployment in the EU15 and limited return flows, suggests that for a substantial share of the labour migrants the gap between standards of living, welfare and job opportunities in Eastern and Western Europe respectively renders it more attractive to stay and make the most out of the situation than returning home. Hence, the old truism that there is nothing as permanent as temporary migration may seem to be confirmed once more. What such a scenario might mean for the social models of the home and host countries is another question, which must take into account the fact that the debt-crisis in the euro-zone has prompted rising emigration from Southern Europe. Germany thus doubled its net inward flow of immigrants in 2011 alone, from 128,000 to 240,000;[54] in addition to workers from Poland and Romania, the numbers arriving from the crisis-stricken southern countries rose sharply. By mid-2012, it was reported that emigration from Spain since early 2011 had passed 1 million. In formerly popular destination countries, like the UK, Ireland and Spain, where austerity and the economic crisis have reduced labour demand, many of the labour migrants probably move on to other destinations – but how many have chosen to stay and attempt to make a living is difficult to estimate.[55] Nonetheless, the likely consequence is that the flows of labour migrants from the eastern and southern EU countries will become more concentrated to the northern parts of Europe where the economic prospects are better.

Discussion: Challenges and Responses

The enlargement of the EU/EFTA labour markets – comprising a workforce of more than 250 million people – has provided substantial gains for the participant states and citizens. Up until the financial crisis, significant economic convergence was witnessed, illustrated by jumps in GDP per capita in PPS from 38.8 to 52.9 per cent; of the average EU15 level in Latvia and from 43.8 to 49.7 per cent in Poland from 2003 to 2007.[56] In common currency, wages in Latvia rose from 12.9 to 18.2 per cent of the EU15 level, and in Poland from 21.5 to 25.4 per cent; that is, roughly one percentage point per year. In Poland, employment rates rose from 51 per cent in 2003 to 59 per cent in 2008, according to Kaczmarczyk, showing that the emigration of redundant labour has had a dynamic effect on domestic labour markets.[57] Although developments after the financial crisis have been more mixed, considerable win–win gains have been reaped. This should not lead to neglect of the challenges associated with transfers of labour in such magnitudes in the receiving as well as in the sending states.

Sound labour migration leading to a better match of capital, labour and skills in the European economy, and a reduction of the wealth and income gap, is certainly beneficial for all, whereas less benign forms of labour migration may have unintended, ambiguous effects. The prototypical 'worst-case' scenario is when scarce, high-skilled employees leave professional jobs in the NMS and take up unskilled, low-productive work in slack Western labour-market segments.[58] For the individual migrant this can be perfectly rational, since pay even well below the going rate can be considerably higher than at home, especially when taking into account earned rights to more generous, portable social benefits (the 'social wage'). For the employer it may imply saved costs and a competitive edge. For the involved states, and for the European economy as a whole, however, the sum (and distribution) of gains and losses may look different. For the sending states, the loss of critical human resources can hamper economic and social development, in contrast to outflows of excess labour, which may reduce imbalances in domestic labour markets and public budgets. Of critical importance for the sending states is thus their ability to benefit from brain gain resulting from circular and return migration of skilled labour in particular.[59] For the receiving states increased competition for low-end jobs may cause substitution effects on the recruitment side, undermine wage floors and engender marginalisation of vulnerable groups (e.g. third country immigrants) as well as higher social expenditures. For the European economy as a whole, the sub-optimal allocation of skills and of productive resources entails a loss in productive capacity and growth, and tends to reproduce regional disparities.

But labour migration can, as pointed out by Meardi, also serve as political voice, as when workers vote with their feet and exit social models they consider irresponsive to worker demands.[60] On the receiving end, workers who perceive the hiring of low-paid migrant labour as a threat to their interests may mobilise political pressure for better labour-market regulation. On the other hand, tax-payers fearing 'social tourism' may support political forces that demand more restrictive social policies or migration policies, as indicated by the rise in support for welfare chauvinist parties in several countries. Without going into the task of weighing the relative shares of 'virtuous' and 'vicious' consequences of the rise in intra-European labour migration, it goes without saying that market forces alone will not provide for optimal social and economic outcomes. Even the European labour market needs regulations and incentives that promote re-allocation of labour in ways that enhance productivity and prevent adjustments which lead to short-sighted, low-cost competition and waste of human resources.

It is for such reasons the EU has developed its rules and conditions for free movement, which stipulate that certain host country rules and conditions shall apply. By preventing employers from hiring migrant and posted labourers on poor terms and in sub-standard conditions, these rules are meant to serve several purposes. First, they aim to protect the social systems of host countries from erosion, and, second, to facilitate a level competition field, where productivity and quality are more important determinants than arbitrary cross-country price differentials. Third, by preventing host countries from establishing low-cost havens where they can link superior, capital-intensive production facilities with cheap migrant labour, the rules can, if properly applied, protect the sending countries against the loss of their comparative cost advantages that are crucial for their ability to attract foreign investment, retain competitiveness and catch up with the richer economies.

In this view, proper labour-market regulations and institutions providing wage levels which are adapted to the particular cost and production structures of each country are essential to facilitate the sound reallocation of investment flows and to ensure that the four freedoms serve the purpose of balanced, upward economic and social convergence. If such institutional regulations evaporate, companies in richer countries can out-compete businesses in less well-off states (even in the niches where they used to enjoy comparative advantages) by linking superior societal and capital endowments with cheap foreign labour and services. In such a context, labour migration will feed the development of a two-tiered labour market in the richer countries. This can in effect pave the way for a pattern of integration in which the poorer countries risk being locked into a role as suppliers of cheap labour and labour intensive goods, while higher value added production remains concentrated in the richer countries.[61] In a demographically ageing Europe, where labour in the coming decades will likely become a scarcity factor, such a scenario is likely to reinforce the regional divergence of economic development highlighted by the debt crisis. As a result, labour migration might well be amplified, enhanced by the next rounds of Balkan country accession. While wealthier countries may benefit economically, their challenge in such a two-tiered Europe is that their labour-market and welfare-state institutions will come under increasing strain and face reinforced economic and political pressures for development of a two-pronged social benefit system in order to handle the resultant dualisation of the labour market.

Given their diverse social models, the member states on the receiving end of the migratory chains have so far developed different responses to protect their labour market and social systems. Organised labour has in most countries stepped up its efforts to extend national wage floors to all workers and called for strengthened enforcement of work-life rules. Reflecting vast differences in union strength and collective bargaining after the past decades' decline, such demands have met with mixed responses from employers and governments.[62] In the crisis-ridden liberal market economies of the UK and Ireland, the deregulated labour markets and minimalist welfare systems imply that adjustments, as in the US, are mostly left to the mechanism of supply and demand, though with the statutory minimum wage as a lower floor. In the continental countries, such as Germany, where the partial deregulation and dualisation of the national labour markets have already come quite far, organised labour has tended to gain government support for broadened extension of collectively agreed minimum wages, supplemented by statutory minima in areas where no such mechanisms exist. The Latin countries have relied on similar means. Apart from Sweden and Denmark, which rely on their strong unions' capacity to strike collective agreements, the Nordic countries have also developed extension mechanisms and strengthened state control measures.

A problem common to all countries in the wake of the Laval Quartet of cases, however, is that the wage floors applied to posted and migrant labour represent minima which are often well below the going rate in respective national industries. They are also very difficult to enforce, given patchy union presence and the fluidity of these segments of the labour market. That labour representatives are curbed from applying collective action against cross-border service providers following the court decision in the Laval case, has not made the task easier, even in better organised sectors. Circumvention, abuse and wage dumping are thus frequently reported, exerting pressure on conditions in the lower rungs of national labour markets. A common concern among European trade unions is thus that the combination of austerity, higher unemployment and the increased migration of labour and posted workers will propel widened wage inequality and further the erosion of industrial relations institutions. As witnessed in the US from the 1980s, such a scenario is likely to accelerate the past decades' weakening of trade unions and tilt the balance of power further in the favour of employers.

Organised employers have adopted very different approaches to these tendencies. In some countries, such as the Netherlands, Denmark and Belgium, employer associations have tended to share the unions' concern with the competitive distortion and undermining of organised companies. In other countries, such as Germany, Sweden and Norway, employers in the manufacturing export sectors have viewed the lowering of costs as a welcome competitive benefit and have opposed union demands – in some instances with consent of the core staff. In domestically oriented sectors, typically construction and cleaning, where low-cost firms often outcompete organised companies, employer federations have tended to support the unions' call for strengthened regulations and enforcement. The issue of labour migration has thus caused division and controversy across traditional lines of conflict in working life.

Although the fears of 'social tourism' have so far proven unfounded, such controversies are accentuated by the two-fold interplay between the welfare state and labour migration.[63] On the one hand, the ailing European welfare states can benefit from migration through increased revenues and supply of labour; on the other hand, they can provide adverse incentive effects in the markets for migrant labour. While social benefits bolster the reservation wage and underpin the bargaining power of workers in the domestic labour market, this function can be reversed in the case of migrant jobseekers. Qualification for portable social benefits with often considerable value in the country of origin can for migrant labour, *ceteris paribus*, create incentives to accept jobs with inferior pay and to remain in the host country in case of joblessness, even if vacant jobs are available in the home country. For employers that rely on short-term hiring of low-paid migrants, sometimes on a casual basis, this mechanism can in effect help companies pass on labour costs to the state and serve as an indirect welfare state subsidy of dubious companies with low productivity, engaged in the precarious hiring of migrant labour. As pointed out by a research-based review committee study appointed by the Norwegian government, such mechanisms underscore the critical interplay between labour-market regulation and welfare-state policies in facilitating sound migration and viable social benefit systems.[64] Adequate measures to prevent social dumping and dualisation in the labour market are therefore, according to the review, a key prerequisite to ensure the sustainability of inclusive welfare states in open labour markets.

The European welfare states will certainly need more immigrant labour to care for the growing elderly population in the years to come, at the same time as social needs increase and revenues decrease in the wake of crisis and austerity. In order to prevent waste of human resources, to secure workers – regardless of origin – the pay and working conditions that enable them to use their skills and maintain self-reliance, and to preserve the welfare state, there is a strong case for the re-embedding of the European labour market. Labour migration is not the problem but certainly a part of the solution, provided that proper labour-market regulations and institutions are re-established. In an open European labour market of 31 states where the past decades' processes of deregulation and institutional decline have widened the gaps in labour protection and power relations, such a reversal of trends is a daunting task that cannot be resolved through national action alone.[65] The creation of a well-functioning European labour market requires development of common European approaches where labour-market and welfare-state policies are considered indispensable and interrelated parts of a coordinated strategy to promote growth, employment and social integration.

Notes

1. The chapter is based on research funded by the Norwegian Ministry of Labour and several projects funded by the Research Council of Norway.
2. Krings, T. 'A Race to the Bottom? Trade Unions, EU Enlargement and the Free Movement of Labour'. *European Journal of Industrial Relations*, 15/1 (2009): 49–69.

3. Hollande, D., Fic, T., Paluchowski, P., Rincon-Aznar, A. and Stokes, L. *Labour Mobility within the EU: The Impact of Enlargement and Transitional Arrangements.* NIESR Discussion Paper No. 379, London, 2011; Kahanec, M. *Labor Mobility in an Enlarged European Union.* IZA Discussion Paper No 6485, Bonn, 2012.

4. Brochmann, G. and Dølvik, J. E. 'Is Immigration an Enemy of the Welfare State? Between Human Rights and Realpolitik in European Immigration Policies'. In D. Papademetriou (ed.) *Europe and its Immigrants in the 21st Century.* Washington, DC: Migration Policy Institute, 2006.

5. Galgóczi, B., Leschke, J. and Watt, A. *Intra-EU Labour Migration: Flows, Effects and Policy Responses.* Working Paper 2009:3, updated 2011. Brussels: ETUI, 2011.

6. Kaczmarczyk, P. *Free Movement of Workers and Labour Market Adjustment. Recent Experiences from OECD Countries and the European Union,* OECD, 2012.

7. Galgóczi et al.: *Intra-EU Labour Migration: Flows, Effects and Policy Responses.*

8. Brücker, H. et al. *Labour Mobility within the EU in the Context of Enlargement and the Functioning of the Transitional Arrangements,* Final report (IAB, CMR, fRDB, GEP, WIFO, wiiw), Nuremberg, 2009; Kahanec: *Labor Mobility in an Enlarged European Union.*

9. Dølvik, J. E. and Visser, J. 'Free movement, Equal Treatment and Worker Rights: Can the EU Solve its Trilemma of Fundamental Principles?' *Industrial Relations Journal,* 2 (2009): 491–509.

10. Brenke, K., Yuksel, M. and Zimmermann, K. F. 'EU Enlargement under Continued Mobility Restrictions: Consequences for the German Labour Market'. In M. Kahanec and K. F. Zimmermann (eds) *EU Labour Markets After Post-Enlargement Migration.* Berlin: Springer, 2010; Brochmann, G. and Hagelund, A. 'Migrants in the Scandinavian Welfare State. The Emergence of a Social Policy Problem'. *Nordic Journal of Migration Research,* 1/1 (2011): 13–24.

11. Kahanec: *Labor Mobility in an Enlarged European Union*; Meardi, G. *Social Failures of EU Enlargement: A Case of Workers Voting with their Feet.* New York: Routledge, 2012.

12. Commons, J. R. 'The American Shoemakers, 1648–1895'. *The Quarterly Journal of Economics*, 24/1 (1909): 39–84.

13. According to Reg 1408/71 labour migrants were entitled to host country benefits from day one, to claim rights earned through work and contributions made in other member states, and to receive such benefits independent of territory of residence, while posted workers remained under the home country regime during the first year of the contract (later altered to the first two years; EC 1612/68 and 1408/71).

14. Streeck, W. and Schmitter, P. C. 'From National Corporatism to Transnational Pluralism: Organized Interests in the Single European Market'. In W. Streeck (ed.) *Social Institutions and Economic Performance.* London: Sage, 1992; Leibfried, S. and Pierson, P. 'Semi-Sovereign Welfare States: Social Policy in a Multitiered Europe'. In S. Leibfried and P. Pierson (eds) *European Social Policy. Between Fragmentation and Integration.* Washington DC: Brookings Institute, 1995.

15. Menz, G. *Varieties of Capitalism and Europeanization. National Response Strategies to the Single Market.* Oxford: Oxford University Press, 2005.

16. EC 96/71.

17. See article 3.1.

18. The Laval Quartet refers to a series of decisions taken by the European Court of Justice regarding the rights member states are allowed to secure posted workers in accordance with the Posting of Workers Directive, and restrictions applying to trade union rights to take industrial action against foreign service providers and companies relocating across borders (Laval C341/05, Viking C-438/05, Rüffert C-346/06, Luxemburg C-319/06).

19. Kahanec: *Labor Mobility in an Enlarged European Union.*

20. Dølvik and Visser: 'Free Movement, Equal Treatment and Worker Rights: Can the EU Solve its Trilemma of Fundamental Principles?', pp. 491–509.

21. Emmenegger, P., Häusermann, S., Palier, B. and Seeleib-Kaiser, M. 'How We Grow Unequal'. In Emmenegger et al. (eds) *The Age of Dualization. The Changing Face of Inequality in Deindustrializing Societies.* Oxford: Oxford University Press, 2012.

22. Meardi: *Social Failures of EU Enlargement: A Case of Workers Voting with their Feet.*

23. The TAs varied from strict quotas in many continental countries to virtually free movement in Denmark and Norway, provided that workers from the NMS were ensured equal conditions. See Boeri, T. and Brücker, H. *Migration, Co-ordination Failures and EU Enlargement.* IZA Discussion Paper No. 1600, 2005.

24. Dølvik and Visser: 'Free Movement, Equal Treatment and Worker Rights: Can the EU Solve its Trilemma of Fundamental Principles?', pp. 491–509.

25. Hollande et al.: *Labour Mobility within the EU: The Impact of Enlargement and Transitional Arrangements*; Kahanec: *Labor Mobility in an Enlarged European Union.*

26. Desiderio, M. V., 'Free Mobility Areas Across OECD: An Overview'. In *Free Movement of Workers and Labour Market Adjustment: Recent Experiences from OECD Countries and the European Union*, OECD 2012.

27. Dølvik, J. E. and Eldring, L. 'Setting Wage Floors in Open Markets. The Social Partners' Role in Europe's Multilevel Governance'. In Evju et al. (eds) *Regulating Transnational Labour in Europe: The Quandaries of Multilevel Governance*, forthcoming 2013.

28. Hollande et al.: *Labour Mobility within the EU: The Impact of Enlargement and Transitional Arrangements.*

29. Reports made for the Commission estimated net outflows of around 3 million during the first 30 years and around 300,000 annually the first years. (Boeri and Brücker: *Migration, Co-ordination Failures and EU Enlargement.*)

30. Brücker et al.: *Labour Mobility within the EU in the Context of Enlargement and the Functioning of the Transitional Arrangements.*

31. Bratsberg, B. and Raaum, O. *Immigration and Wages: Evidence from Construction.* CReAM Discussion Paper Series No. 06/10, 2010; Blanchflower, D. G. and Lawton, H. 'The Impact of Recent Expansion of the EU on the UK Labour Market'. in M. Kahanec and K. F. Zimmermann (eds) *EU Labour Markets After Post-Enlargement Migration.* Berlin: Springer, 2010.

32. Kahanec: *Labor Mobility in an Enlarged European Union.*

33. Kadziauskas, G. 'Lithuanian Migration: Causes, Impacts and Policy Guidelines'. In J. Smith-Bozel (ed.) *Labor Mobility in the European Union: New Members, New Challenges.* Washington DC: Center for European Policy Analysis, 2007; Kaczmarczyk, P. and Okolski, M. *Economic Impacts of Migration on Poland and the Baltic States.* Fafo Working Paper 2008:1. Oslo: Fafo, 2008; Kureková, L. *From Job Search to Skill Search. Political Economy of Labor Migration in Central and Eastern Europe.* PhD dissertation, Central European University, CEU, Budapest, 2011; World Bank. *Labor Markets in EU8+2: From the Shortage of Jobs to the Shortage of Skilled Workers.* Regular Economic Report, Part II: Special Topic. Washington DC, 2007.

34. Galgóczi et al.: *Intra-EU Labour Migration: Flows, Effects and Policy Responses.*

35. Kaczmarczyk: *Free Movement of Workers and Labour Market Adjustment. Recent Experiences from OECD Countries and the European Union.*

36. Interviews with Research Director Alf Vanags, Biceps Institute, Riga, and Professor Morten Hansen, Stockholm Business School Riga, *Aftenposten*, 24 March 2012. Both expect the outflows to continue for a couple of years more. The consequence, according to Alf Vanags, 'crudely put, [is] that only the children and the elderly stay home'.

37. Hazans, M. 'Selectivity of Migrants from Baltic Countries Before and After Enlargement and Responses to the Crisis'. In B. Galgóczi, J. Lescke and A. Watt (eds) *EU Labour Migration in Troubled Times:*

Skills Mismatch, Return, and Policy Responses. Farnham: Ashgate, 2012.

38. *Aftenposten*, 24 March 2012; Galgóczi et al.: *Intra-EU Labour Migration: Flows, Effects and Policy Responses*.

39. Alf Vanags and Morten Hansen, *Aftenposten*, 24 March 2012.

40. Friberg, J. H. and Eldring, L. *Polonia i Oslo 2010. Mobilitet, arbeid og levekår blant polakker i hovedstaden*. Fafo Working Paper 2011:13. Oslo: Fafo, 2011.

41. Statistics Norway. *Innvandring og innvandrere*. Oslo: Statistics Norway, 2012. http://www.ssb.no/emner/00/00/10/innvandring.

42. Dølvik and Visser: 'Free Movement, Equal Treatment and Worker Rights: Can the EU Solve its Trilemma of Fundamental Principles?', pp. 491–509.

43. EC–European Commission. Proposal for a Council Regulation on the Exercise of the Right to Take Collective Action Within the Context of the Freedom of Establishment and the Freedom to Provide Services. COM, 130/3 (2012).

44. EC–European Commission. 'Geographical Mobility in the Context of EU Enlargement'. In *Employment in Europe*. Luxemburg: Official Publications of the European Communities (2008).

45. van Houk, A. and Houwerzijl, M. *Comparative Study of the Legal Aspects of the Posting of Workers. Executive Summary*. European Commission Conference on Fundamental Social Rights and Posting of Workers in the Framework of the Single Market, Brussels, pp. 27–28, June 2011.

46. Pacolet, J. and De Wispelaere, F. 'Belgium'. In J. Cremers (ed.) *In Search of Cheap Labour in Europe. Working and Living Conditions of Posted Workers*. Brussels: CLR/International, 2011.

47. Bratsberg, B., Dølvik, J. E. and Raaum, O. 'Economic Shocks, the Legal Environment and Work-related Migration'. Paper presented at Inside-Move, NORFACE, CReAM:VI Workshop on *Migration and Labor Economics* (IAE-CSIC), Barcelona, 18–19 October 2012.

48. Ødegaard, A. M. and Andersen, R. *Østeuropeisk arbeidskraft i hotell, verft, fiskeindustri og kjøttindustri.* Fafo Working Paper 2011:21. Oslo: Fafo, 2011; Lillie, N. 'Transnational Work and the Consequences of Restructuring: Evidence from Construction and Ship-Building Industries in Finland'. Paper presented at the 2010 IREC Conference: Industrial Relations and Labour Market Governance during Crisis, Oslo: Fafo, 8–10 September 2010; Lefebvre, B. 'Posted Workers in France'. *Transfer*, 12/2 (2006): 197–213.

49. Lillie, N. and Greer, I. 'Industrial Relations, Migration, and Neoliberal Policies: The Case of the European Construction Sector'. *Politics & Society*, 35/4 (2007): 551–81; Hansen, J. A. and Andersen, S. K. *East European Workers in the Building and Construction Industry*. FAOS Working Paper, Department of Sociology, University of Copenhagen, 2008; Lillie: 'Transnational Work and the Consequences of Restructuring: Evidence from Construction and Ship-Building Industries in Finland'.

50. Dølvik, J. E. and Martin, A. 'Social Model Change and Labour Market Outcomes Before the Crisis: A Comparative Overview'. In J. E. Dølvik and A. Martin (eds) *European Social Models Faced With Crisis*, forthcoming 2013.

51. Friberg and Eldring: *Polonia i Oslo 2010. Mobilitet, arbeid og levekar blant polakker i hovedstaden.*

52. EC–European Commission. Employment and Social Situation Quarterly Review: December 2011. *Memo*, 12/3 (2011).

53. According to Kahanec et al., Western Europe thus saw a 50 per cent drop in immigration from Ukraine, Belarus, Russia and Turkey in 2004–6. Kahanec, M., Zaiceva, A. and Zimmermann, K. F. 'Lessons from Migration after EU Enlargement'. In M. Kahanec and K. F. Zimmermann (eds) *EU Labour Markets After Post-Enlargement Migration*. Berlin: Springer, 2010.

54. *Herald Tribune*, 30 April 2012.

55. Reports from Ireland suggest that those migrants that have earned social benefits rights tend to stay. See Krings, T., Bobek, A., Moriarty, E., Salamonska, J. and Wickham, J. 'Migration and

Recession: Polish Migrants in Post-Celtic Tiger Ireland'. *Sociological Research Online*, 14/2 (2009): 9. http://www.socresonline.org.uk/14/2/9.html.~doi:10.5153/sro.1927; Koehler, J., Laczko, F., Aghazarm, C. and Schad, J. *Migration and the Economic Crisis in the European Union: Implications for Policy*. Brussels: IOM, Thematic Study, 2010.

56. Galgóczi et al.: *Intra-EU Labour Migration: Flows, Effects and Policy Responses.*

57. Kaczmarczyk: *Free Movement of Workers and Labour Market Adjustment. Recent Experiences from OECD Countries and the European Union.*

58. Galgóczi et al.: *Intra-EU Labour Migration: Flows, Effects and Policy Responses.*

59. Kahanec: *Labor Mobility in an Enlarged European Union.*

60. Meardi: *Social Failures of EU Enlargement: A Case of Workers Voting with their Feet.*

61. As pointed out by Meardi (2012), such a scenario bears resemblance with the American path of development, where the articulation of modes of production between extremely advanced, high-cost industries interacting with low-cost, labour-intensive suppliers of ancillary services and sub-deliveries has created a multi-tiered labour market with extreme income inequalities. The difference, however, is that while Europe boldly has opened the labour market between the high- and low-cost member states, the USA, within the NAFTA regime, maintains strict immigration control vis-à-vis Mexico and other states. There is indeed forceful 'regime-competition' among the various US states, but that in contrast to that in the EU, the US Federal budget provides for substantial inter-state fiscal transfers and automatic stabilisers. These similarities and contrasts do indeed underscore the case for preservation of proper systems of labour-market regulation both within and between the member states.

62. Dølvik, J. E., Eldring L. and Visser, J. 'Setting Wage Floors in Open Markets. Europe's Multilevel Governance in Practice'. Paper presented at the FORMULA Conference 'Free Movement, Labour

Market Regulation and Multilevel Governance in an Enlarged
EU/EEA', Oslo, 22–23 March 2013.

63. Kahanec: *Labor Mobility in an Enlarged European Union.*
64. NOU (2011) *Velferd og migrasjon: Den norske modellens framtid,*
p. 7.
65. Dølvik and Martin: *European Social Models Faced With Crisis.*

Further Reading

Aale, P. K. and Moe, I. 'Lengter hjem, blir i Norge'. *Aftenposten* (24
March 2012).

International Herald Tribune. 'Germany Reaches South to Fill Need
for Workers'. *International Herald Tribune*, 30 April 2012.

NOU (2012) *Utenfor og Innenfor. Norges avtaler med EU*, p. 2.

CHAPTER 3

Migration and Welfare Sustainability: The Case of Norway

Grete Brochmann and Anne Skevik Grødem

The development of the Norwegian welfare model largely came about in the period after the Second World War, the basic features having been put in place by the late 1960s. During this period immigration to Norway was close to insignificant. The model, both pragmatic and idealistic, was formed from an early stage as a comprehensive social insurance system, although its rationale was wider. In many ways the model can be seen as a grand societal integration project with three central ingredients: democracy, modernisation and citizenship. A national homogenisation process took place after the war devastation and in tandem with the generation of the welfare state; this is usually seen as the foundation for the required generalised solidarity of the model, as well as its continued popular support and legitimacy. The nation building that in practice came out of these processes fortified and consolidated the ties between territory, central institutions and cultural identities.[1]

The Norwegian welfare model[2] provides comprehensive cover for the range of social needs it tries to satisfy. It is institutionalised around the social rights that give all citizens – in practice, all legal residents – a right to a decent standard of living. It is both solidaristic and universal, in the sense that welfare policy serves the entire population, not just particularly exposed groups. The model turns many of life's risks over to the state, lightening the load of the family for care obligations.[3] It is service-intensive, with local governments playing key roles by providing welfare services. Women's employment levels are high and social consumption is sizeable, as is the level of taxation.

The Norwegian welfare model is furthermore structurally linked to the highly centralised organisation of working life. The regulation of the labour market via collective agreements, tripartite cooperation, active labour-market policies and welfare security throughout life has contributed to productive economies with good flexibility and a high human capital. Working life and welfare have represented mutual supports and buffers, with a high rate of employment to finance welfare and reduce public spending.

Income security has served as a fundamental pillar in this context, both in the form of *social assistance* and *social insurance*. The system, which was designed to constitute a basic safety net for all citizens from cradle to grave, has been generous and therefore also costly, while contributing to the state's ownership of one of the world's most equal income distributions.[4] Both the state and labour unions have influenced social change and development through an institutionalised system of industrial relations. State control and planning have constituted major ingredients in the system, which is essentially tax-based. *Equal treatment* is a key tenet of the system, and the only criterion for accessing the basic income security system is *legal residency*. The welfare model has had a significant standing in the Norwegian population over the decades, with new governments adjusting policies rather than drastically reforming the baselines.

Though migration was not a concern for early welfare architects, the welfare model definitely played a part when an immigration policy was put in place in the mid-1970s. A dual policy approach has been seen as necessary: first, it has been essential to control immigration to the country. The welfare model, all-embracing and generous in principle, risked being undermined if exposed to too great a load, and has had to carry out selection and limitation in relation to potential new members from outside. Second, it has been seen as necessary to integrate new arrivals – especially in working life and also in society. If one is to maintain the societal framework, new members must be made a part of it. Good welfare states do not want to have large numbers of people or groups that fall through the safety net, disturb regulated working life, burden social budgets or eventually undermine solidarity.

Both these preconditions for the governance of immigration in Norway have proven difficult to fully achieve. When the immigration regulation of 1975 was implemented, restrictions on low-skilled labour from the 'South' were a central concern. In the years since, the vast majority of incoming immigrants has thus been people legitimised on humanitarian grounds – refugees and family migrants. After the EU extension in 2004, the largest influx has consisted of labour migrants from the new member states in Eastern and Central Europe. Thus, since the 1970s the preconditions for influx control have been significantly influenced by the development of Human Rights Legislation and after 2004, the obligations related to the EEA agreement.[5] When it comes to the question of integration, the challenges have slowly materialised after the size of the influx increased drastically the last 20 years, highlighting some structural vulnerabilities of the model, particularly related to low-skilled labour.

The Norwegian labour market has a compressed wage structure, which implies that low-skilled work is relatively well paid, whereas high-skilled work is accordingly paid modestly in a relative sense. This wage profile, in combination with a generous and fairly easily accessible welfare system, makes Norway more attractive for the kinds of immigrants that *may* pose a challenge to the basic structure of the model itself. Features of the Norwegian social welfare system can influence immigrant adaptation and integration once they arrive: the combination of high entry-level wages and generous social benefits means that the access to the labour market may be difficult for low-productivity labour. Given the additional very high marginal tax rates, incentives to take up employment may be limited.

The Norwegian welfare model is characterised by an 'institutional equilibrium', whereby features of the well-regulated labour market and the comprehensive welfare state mutually reinforce each other. Immigration and emigration, internal and external to the EEA, may upset this institutional balance. This apprehension added to the general concern about the long-term sustainability of the welfare model due to demographic prospects and the ageing of society, and prompted the centre-left Stoltenberg government to appoint an independent expert commission in 2009. The mandate was to undertake a comprehensive analysis of future sustainability of the Norwegian welfare model in light of increased migration in both directions, and questions pertaining to the effectiveness and impact of integration policies, and questions of popular support and political legitimacy.[6] In the remainder of this chapter, we review the arguments of the committee regarding access to benefits, employment rates and use of social benefits in various immigrant groups in Norway, and additionally present the Committee's proposals designed to make the Norwegian welfare model more sustainable in relation to increased migration. To our knowledge, no other European countries have commissioned a similar investigation. We therefore argue that the conclusions of the committee, while directed at the Norwegian government, are relevant for an international audience.

Access to Social Benefits

Even though the Norwegian welfare model is both universalistic and residence-based, there are eligibility rules that represent barriers to full and immediate access for newcomers.[7] As a main rule, all social benefits in Norway require a period of contribution, or a period of residence in Norway. For instance, in order to have access to the minimum old-age pension, a person must have lived in Norway for three years. In order to have access to the full amount, the recipient must have lived in Norway for 40 years. Similar rules apply to disability pension. For unemployment insurance and sickness leave, the recipient must have been in employment for certain minimum periods. The 'universal' welfare state in all its facets is therefore not extended to immigrants right away. Refugees are privileged and treated as if they had always lived in Norway with regard to social security eligibility. The eligibility rules therefore do not apply to this group, as long as they are residents in Norway. Immigrants from third countries who do not have status as refugees may have limited access to some benefits; for instance, people who have arrived in Norway late in life will only qualify for a small amount of old age pension.

The social security coordination rules of the European Union required all EU/EEA countries to treat EU citizens as nationals for the purposes of social security. This implies that EU citizens can combine contribution periods in their native country and in Norway when being considered for Norwegian social security benefits. For instance, a person must have worked for a minimum of four weeks in order to be eligible for sickness pay. An EU citizen who has worked four weeks or more in his or her native country (or another EU country) need only do one day's work in Norway in order to be eligible. Rights to old age pension and disability pension are acquired after one year in Norway, and the right to full pensions depends on combined eligibility periods in Norway and other EEA countries. Similar conditions apply to the receipt of family benefits, such as the child benefit and the cash-for-care benefit. Child benefit is paid in respect of children under 18, while the cash-for-care benefit is paid for children between the ages of one and two who are not in a publicly sponsored nursery. Both benefits can be exported within the EEA, and will be paid in respect of children living in another EEA country who have a parent working in Norway.

The only benefit that can be claimed by all residents in Norway, irrespective of period of residence and employment record, is social assistance. Unlike almost all other cash benefits, social assistance is financed and administered by the local municipalities; it is means-tested, discretionary and generally seen as a benefit of the last resort. Newly arrived immigrants and immigrants with no work record tend to be channelled to social assistance. This burdens local municipalities with extra costs when accepting new refugees, and it is also seen as unfortunate because the benefit carries a certain stigma. These considerations formed part of the background to the introduction, in the last decade, of two special programmes for newly arrived immigrants and people with short residence. First, newly arrived refugees and their family members have, since 2004, had a right and an obligation to participate in the 'Introduction' programme, which provides an introduction to Norwegian language and society as well as a qualifying course for paid employment. Participants receive an individual salary, which is normally paid at a higher level than social assistance. Second, a special benefit was introduced in 2006 for persons older than 67 years with short periods of residence in Norway, guaranteeing them an income similar to the minimum old age pension. This benefit is paid on stricter conditions than regular old age pension; most importantly, residents cannot stay outside Norway for more than 90 days per year.

A welfare model with residence-based entitlements, and with relatively generous benefits, may be difficult to sustain in periods of elevated migration. National legislation includes clauses that limit some entitlements for persons who have stayed in Norway only for short periods, but these clauses can be bypassed by EU regulations for EU citizens. Comprehensive intra-EU migration is as yet a relatively new phenomenon, and it remains to be seen how severe this challenge is for the Norwegian welfare model. The persons arriving through the humanitarian channels often have difficulties getting employed – at least in the short run – but they have not got access *in order to* contribute to the Norwegian economy. The challenge to the overall economy nevertheless depends on their employability.

Labour-Market Participation

Labour-market participation rates are generally high in Norway, when compared to other countries in the EEA. This is particularly true for women and older workers (between 55 and 64 years of age).[8] Overall, 78 per cent of men and 75 per cent of women in Norway were in employment in 2009 (those between 15 and 64 years). Figure 3.1 shows employment rate by age for the population at large, and for various immigrant groups in Norway, as a percentage of all residents aged 15 to 61 from the respective region. Employment rates for the over-60s are omitted because there are very few immigrants from Central and Eastern Europe and non-Western countries within this age group in Norway. The figure illustrates that labour-market participation rates are high in the majority population, close to 90 per cent for people at prime working age. Immigrants from other Western countries have almost as high participation rates, while the rates for immigrants from EU member states in Central and Eastern Europe are somewhat lower. The consistently lowest rates are, however, found among immigrants from non-Western countries.

Within the main regions, there are vast variations in employment rates for immigrants from different countries. For example, immigrants from Chile and Sri Lanka have employment rates of around 70 per cent, which is almost as high as the majority population, while

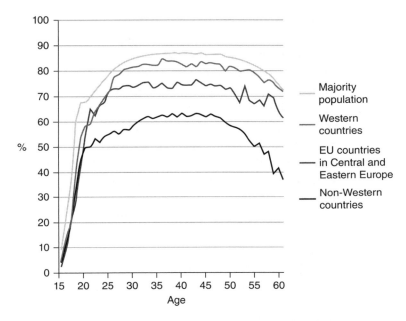

FIGURE 3.1 Employment rates by immigrant status, region of origin and age. Norway, fourth quarter 2009.
Source: Statistics Norway, analysis commissioned by the Welfare and Migration Committee.

immigrants from Somalia and Iraq have employment rates of 32 and 43 per cent respectively. Furthermore, those who have arrived as refugees tend to have the lowest employment rates, while labour migrants – unsurprisingly – have the highest. Family migrants as a group have higher employment rates than refugees, but lower rates than labour migrants. Increased family migration best explains why the employment rate for immigrants from EU countries in Central and Eastern European is lower than for the majority population for all age groups: newly arrived family migrants from these countries have very low employment rates (44 per cent). Employment rates within this category, however, increase rapidly to 71 per cent for those who have resided in Norway for five to nine years, and seem to remain at this relatively high level.

Employment rates also vary by period of residence, increasing in most groups for the first 10 to 15 years. Some evidence, however, indicates that employment rates level off and then begin to fall after this initial period of increase. A much-quoted study followed the labour migrants who arrived before 1975 over the course of their lives, and compared their employment rates to those of a similar group of men from the majority population.[9] At the beginning of the period, the employment rates of the labour migrants exceeded those of the reference group, but after about ten years, employment rates fell rapidly. By 2007, which was the last year of observation, only about 30 per cent of the labour migrants were in employment. The analysis has later been repeated for groups who arrived later – family migrants and refugees – and while the results are mixed, and observation periods sometimes are short, many groups seem to follow a similar pattern: employment rates increase rapidly in the first 10 to 15 years, then level off and sometimes fall.

Descendants of immigrants in Norway are still a relatively young group. In early 2010, there were 93,000 descendants living in Norway, of whom only about 25 per cent were older than 15 years. Norwegian-born descendants of immigrants above 20 have lower employment rates than their peers in the majority population, but higher than immigrants in similar age groups.[10] This is true for both men and women.

Use of Social Benefits

Employment rates are reflected in the mirror of welfare benefit use. People of working age who aren't providing for themselves in the labour market will either be taken care of by the family, or receive some form of social benefit. When looking at cross-sectional data, immigrants as a group have a lower consumption of social benefits than the native population.[11] There are several reasons for this. First, very few immigrants in Norway are old enough to qualify for old age pension. In addition, immigrants from Central and Eastern Europe come in order to work, and therefore typically spend relatively short periods of residence in Norway, and in many cases do not come in contact with (and may not be well informed about) the benefits system. Finally, many benefits in Norway require a previous work record, and are not available to people outside the labour force. This is one reason why, for instance, immigrant women from non-Western countries are far less likely to receive sickness pay than women in the majority population. Patterns change, however, as immigrants grow older, and more immigrants have longer periods of residence in Norway.

There has been considerable concern for quite a while in Norway about the use of social benefits among immigrants from non-Western countries. In recent years, worries have also come to the fore about the use of benefits by immigrants from Central and Eastern Europe. Concerns about these two categories differ, however, with anxiety over the latter group linked to the speedy access to certain benefits that EU migrants receive (see above), and to the question of the exportability of these benefits, once immigrants leave the country again. Because Norway is a high-cost country, benefit export can be a lucrative opportunity for workers from countries like Poland and Lithuania. The Welfare and Migration Committee has estimated that one cash-for-care allowance makes up half an average wage in Poland, which indicates that access to this benefit is highly beneficial for individuals who work in Norway, and whose children reside in Poland. Benefit exports to countries in Central and Eastern Europe more than doubled between 2004 and 2008, but still make up only one per cent of total benefit exports from Norway.[12] The rapid increase in this short period of time, however, indicates the potential for future developments. While these insights have raised some eyebrows in Norway, it must be emphasised that this benefit export is legal according to EU law.

Non-Western immigrants are clearly over-represented among the recipients of the social assistance benefit in Norway, and have been so for a very long time. This is the kind of assistance any legal immigrant can access without prior work, and prior to the onset of the introduction programme (see above), it used to be the predominant kind of support for refugees. Approximately 12 per cent of immigrants from non-Western countries received social assistance in 2008, compared to 3 per cent of the majority population. Immigrants also received the benefit for longer periods: 47 per cent of the immigrants receiving social assistance had done so for six months or more, compared to 37 per cent of the recipients in the general population. The proportion of immigrants in receipt of social assistance decreases with increasing periods of residence. This is partly because more immigrants become self-sufficient over time, but also partly because recipients are transferred to other benefits.[13]

The rates of disability pensioning have generally increased in Norway over the last decades. The reasons for this are unclear, as a general decline in public health has not been documented. Rates of disability pensioning increase with age, which is part of the reason why immigrants, as a group, are less likely to receive disability pension than the majority population – the average immigrant is younger than the average person in the majority population. The studies quoted above, which documented the rapid decline in employment rates for labour migrants after about ten years in Norway, also documented a corresponding increase in disability pensioning. After about 30 years, two out of three of the early labour migrants were in receipt of some form of disability pension, in comparison to one in three from the reference group. Similar trends are found for immigrant cohorts who arrived later.[14] There is no single explanation for this pattern. Competing explanations include the incentive structure of the disability pension, characteristics of the labour-market segments where immigrants typically work, and discrimination. The empirical observations, however, galvanised the debate about the sustainability of the Norwegian welfare state in light of increasing immigration.

Norway is unusual in the OECD area in having a rights-based, subsistence-level benefit, targeted exclusively at lone parents (the transitional allowance). The benefit is income-tested, and can be paid without further conditions until the youngest child is three years old. Female immigrants from Somalia have a disproportionately high use of this benefit. Of all Somali women who arrived in Norway between 1989 and 1993 and had children under three, 74 per cent had, at some point in time, received transitional allowance.[15] Other immigrant groups, including Pakistanis and Turks, used this benefit only to a very small extent.

The uses of social benefits vary widely between different immigrant groups. The variations observed can have different explanations, linked to the opportunity structures that face immigrants with short- or longer-term residence in Norway. Cultural parameters may also play a part. Very little, however, is known about these dynamics.

Legitimacy of the Welfare State

Will increasing immigration, and a more ethnically diverse society, undermine public support for social welfare arrangements? Whilst there is some evidence for this from the USA, the connection between immigration and support for the welfare state as such appears to be weak or non-existent in Europe.[16] Some scholars have pointed out, however, that even if the general backing for welfare arrangements remains high, there may be support for limiting these arrangements exclusively to natives. One review article, for example, pointed out a stable proportion of Europeans arguing that the state should un- questionably be responsible for health care and 'a decent standard of living for the elderly'. Yet this coexists with weakening support for statements, as to governmental responsibility for 'a decent stan- dard of living for the unemployed', 'providing a job for everyone who wants one' and 'reducing income differences between the rich and the poor'.[17] This suggests that there is no reduction in support for measures people assume they themselves will need one day, but there is weakening support for measures targeted at 'others'.

In Norway, three different surveys have picked up a certain support for a 'two-track' welfare state which reserves key benefits and services for natives. For instance, 39 per cent disagreed with the statement, 'Refugees and immigrants should have the same right to social as- sistance as Norwegians, even if they are not Norwegian citizens'.[18] In another survey, conducted in 2009, 32 per cent agreed fully or partly with the statement, 'People born in Norway should be given priority over immigrants in access to public welfare'.[19] And in the European Social Survey in Norway, 39 per cent expressed the opinion that immigrants should only gain full access to the Norwegian benefit system when they became Norwegian citizens.[20] Finally, a survey published in 2006 asked people in Norway how they felt about intro- ducing a basic income, which would be an expensive socio-political reform. After responding, those in favour were asked if they would still support this reform if it also included non-citizens, while those against were asked if they would still be against if the basic income was paid to Norwegian citizens only. Thirty-two per cent of the respondents changed their mind when immigrants or non-citizen were taken out of the prospective pool of recipients of the benefit. While there is no systematic evidence for lowered support for the welfare state in Norway, there is clearly a certain support for a 'two-track' design that gives lower benefits to newcomers or non-citizens. It is worth noting that since the publication of the report from the Welfare and Migration Commission, the right-wing Progress Party has repeatedly stated that they will look into the opportunity for restricting social benefits in Norway to Norwegian citizens only. Introducing this principle for EEA citizens will almost certainly be a breach with EU law, but there is more leeway when facing immigrants from third countries.

The Future of the Norwegian Welfare State

The Norwegian welfare model faces a combination of challenges: the ageing population will limit the growth of the labour force in the decades ahead. If the immigrant population does not enter work and stay in work at a level closer to that of the majority population, this will add to the future financial problems, and it would also most likely spur political tension over the funding and distribution of the welfare goods. On the other hand, if immigrants work at the same or a higher degree than the majority, their presence will contribute to the conservation of the welfare state. The Welfare and Migration Committee therefore argued that migration policy, employment and integration policies, as well as welfare policy, must be approached in context.

Curtailing immigration to a greater degree than is already in operation today is not among the recommendations of the Commission. This is partly because Norway, like most other countries in Europe, is restrained by international conventions and agreements regarding the governing of immigration, leaving little leeway for more restrictive policies. In the areas that are handled by national policies, Norwegian practices are already relatively strict. Moreover, the Committee wished to emphasise that immigration as such is not necessarily a problem – the problem is immigration to non-employment. The emphasis was therefore on integration and welfare policies.

The Welfare and Migration Committee identified two key issues to be addressed if the Norwegian welfare state is to remain sustainable in its present form: first, the mass influx of workers from other EEA countries presents the labour market with new challenges. There is a risk that a second-tier labour market will develop, fuelling labour from poorer countries, working for lower wages and under poorer working conditions. This could alter the dynamics of the labour market significantly, potentially also changing the relationship between the labour market and the welfare state. EEA citizens who work in Norway, no matter how poorly paid, will acquire welfare rights in Norway. Costs will then be shifted from employers to the public purse, with potentially significant effects on public budgets. The Welfare and Migration Committee argued that the best way to avoid this cost switching is to continue ongoing efforts to avoid the development of both a second-tier labour market and 'social dumping'. The Committee further pointed out that benefit exports are legitimate, and that benefit recipients have a right to live where they choose. The potential problem, however, is that the opportunity to export benefits can make them more attractive and may recruit more users. In Norway, most people will have a higher disposable income as full-time workers than as recipients of social benefits. If the benefit can be exported to a low-cost country, many people can attain a higher living standard as emigrated benefit-recipients than they would have as full-time workers in Norway.

The second main challenge for the welfare model is the relatively low employment rates and early exit from the labour market, documented among immigrants from non-Western countries. As the numbers of immigrants from third countries are also likely to continue growing in the future, some structural adjustments in the welfare model seem necessary to accommodate the problem.

There are features of the Norwegian welfare model that make it particularly vulnerable when exposed to certain kinds of immigration,

as we have seen. One response to this challenge is welfare-state retrenchment – that is, lower and more targeted benefits. This would
undermine the Norwegian welfare model as it has historically been
known, and move Norway closer to the Anglo-American model of
welfare. An alternative is to abandon the universalist approach in
favour of a differentiated approach, where the most generous and
extensive protection is reserved for citizens or long-term residents. As
the previous section indicates, there is some support for this approach
among the Norwegian population. Yet such a layered line would easily
disturb the basic mechanisms of the very welfare/labour nexus, thus
serving to weaken its functions – in the long run also for the majority:
a two-track system of welfare entitlements would gradually serve to
pressurise wages below the 'floor' established in relation to the main
welfare level of the economy. The development of a low-paid, second-
tier labour market could in turn push welfare benefits even lower, in
order to ensure that work pays. The risk is a downward spiral, what
Barth and Moene have called 'the inequality multiplier', representing
a significant departure from the basic equal treatment policy of the
residence-based welfare model.[21]

The answer to the mixed challenges related to increasing mobility in
and out of the territory is to adjust the model to ensure its sustainability
under new conditions. This seems necessary in order to avoid the
'levelling down' of social protection for the whole population. An
integrated approach to this is pertinent, using combined methods
relating to labour-market parameters and the formation of welfare
entitlements, as well as ensuring immigration and integration policies
are being linked in cohesive ways.

The core endeavour is to promote the employability of the newcomers. This means reinvigorating the 'work-line' approach in order
to stimulate employment of more people or, in other words, to raise
the employment level of the less productive layers of the population,
through public investment in their human capital. A substantial effort
has to be made to have more people participate in the workforce according to their skill level and personal preconditions, bringing them
off passive cash transfers. Three different factors need to be taken into
consideration: the skill enhancement, activation and facilitation.

Two main policy directions have been recommended which can handle both the benefit export concern and the problem of low employment rates: an activation policy and an increased emphasis on *the provision of services* in lieu of cash benefits. The committee proposes a far more active use of graded sickness and disability benefits, suggesting that people should only be declared '100 per cent unable to work' in extreme cases. This would encourage employment among those resident in Norway, and it would decrease exports simply because exportable benefits would be smaller. Prioritising services over cash benefits will also limit export because services are physically linked to the territory. As an example of this approach, the committee proposed to phase out the cash-for-care benefit, and instead give former recipients priority to publicly sponsored childcare. Securing access to services and leisure activities for children and young people, regardless of their family income, may also help prevent the transfer of marginalisation from one generation to the next.

Regarding the activation of skills, there is no way to bypass the process of increasing the basic qualifications of low-skilled immigrants. Language skills and knowledge of the functioning of Norwegian society must to be conveyed from an early stage. The introduction programme for newly arrived immigrants has delivered promising results, but it can be fine-tuned further in terms of better tailoring to the very diverse individual needs, and in terms of qualifying users for the labour market. The programme can also be extended to groups who are not in the target group today, after an assessment of the individual needs.

Activation and increased service provision are, however, not easy solutions. Heavy investment in qualification programmes and possibly subsidised employment will be necessary. A central element in the activation (or work-oriented welfare reform) approach is to create sufficient demand for labour. And as employers have received an abundant supply of workers since 2004 from the new member countries, this premise is at risk for low-skilled, vulnerable labour in the internal market. Consequently, the state will have to subsidise and facilitate the entry of such groups into employment, and possibly also their continued participation. Innovative measures should be targeted at employers, to reduce the risk of employing persons with low, or unknown, skills.

Enjoying a strong economy with an advanced welfare state, Norway is an attractive prospect for potential immigrants. Immigration represents an opportunity for the economy, contribution to an enlarged labour force, varied competences and greater flexibility in the labour market. In order to realise this possibility, however, it is necessary to facilitate the inclusion of newcomers in productive labour to a larger extent than currently exists today. The Norwegian welfare model represents both a problem and a solution in this respect.

Notes

1. See Brochmann, G. and Hagelund, A. *Velferdens grenser. Innvandringspolitikk og velferdsstat i Skandinavia 1945–2010*. Oslo: Universitetsforlaget, 2010.

2. See Kildal, N. and Kuhnle, S. (eds) *Normative Foundations of the Welfare State: The Nordic Experience*. London: Routledge, 2005.

3. Sejersted, F. *Sosialdemokratiets tidsalder: Norge og Sverige i det 20. århundre.* Oslo: Pax, 2005.

4. Barth, E., Moene, K. and Wallerstein, M. *Equality under Pressure. Challenges for the Scandinavian Model of Distribution.* Oslo: Gyldendal Norsk Forlag, 2003.

5. Norway is not an EU member country, but has for all practical purposes the same rights and duties related to the internal market, through the European Economic Area agreement.

6. The Commission (headed by Grete Brochmann, author of this chapter. Anne Skevik Groedem was a central part of the secretariat) delivered its report on 10 May 2011. Available at http://www.regjeringen.no/upload/BLD/IMA/nou_2011_7_ perspective_andsummary.pdf.

7. The rules governing access to Norwegian benefits are more fully described in NOU 2011:7, Velferd og migrasjon. Den norske modellens framtid. (Welfare and Migration: The Norwegian

model's future.) Available at http://www.regjeringen.no/nb/dep/bld/dok/nouer/2011/nou-2011-07.html?id=642496.

8. Europe in figures. Eurostat year book 2010. ISSN 1681-4789. Available at http://epp.eurostat.ec.europa.eu/portal/page/portal/product_details/publication?p_product_code=KS-CD-10-220.

9. Bratsberg, B., Raaum, O. and Røed, K. 'When Minority Labor Migrants Meet the Welfare State'. *Journal of Labor Economics*, 28/3 (2010): 633–76; see also Bratsberg, B., Raaum, O. and Røed, K. *Yrkesdeltaking på lang sikt blant ulike innvandergrupper i Norge*. The Frisch Centre Report no. 1/2011. Oslo: Frisch Centre, 2011.

10. Olsen, B. 'Unge med innvandrerbakgrunn i arbeid og utdanning'. Statistics Norway Report no. 9. Oslo: Statistics Norway, 2010.

11. Løwe, T. 'Innvandreres bruk av velferdsytelser 2009. Mottak av 16 typer trygdeytelser blant ulike innvandrergrupper'. Statistics Norway Report no. 7. Oslo: Statistics Norway, 2011.

12. NOU 2011:7, Velferd og migrasjon. Den norske modellens framtid, Chapter 10.

13. Hirsch, A. A. *Sosialhjelpsmottakere blant innvandrere 1999–2002, 2005–2008*. Statistics Norway Report no. 35. Oslo: Statistics Norway, 2010.

14. Bratsberg et al.: *Yrkesdeltaking på lang sikt blant ulike innvandergrupper i Norge*.

15. Bratsberg et al.: *Yrkesdeltaking på lang sikt blant ulike innvandergrupper i Norge*.

16. See, for example, Senik, C., Stichnoth, H. and van der Straten, K. 'Immigration and natives' Attitudes towards the Welfare State: Evidence from the European Social Survey'. *Social Indicators Research*, 91/3 (2009): 345–70.

17. Miller, D. 'Multiculturalism and the Welfare State: Theoretical Reflections'. In K. Banting and W. Kymlicka (eds) *Multiculturalism and the Welfare State: Recognition and Redistribution in Contemporary Democracies*. Oxford: Oxford University Press, 2006.

18. Aardal, B., Høstmark, M., Lagerstrøm, B. O. and Stavn, G. *Valgunderskelsen 2005. Dokumentasjon- og tabellrapport.* Report 31/2007. Statistics Norway, 2005.

19. Oslo: IMDi. *Integreringsbarometeret 2009. Holdninger til innvandring, integrering og mangfold.* IMDi Report no. 4–2010.

20. OECD. *Migration Outlook 2010.* Paris: OECD, 2010.

21. See Barth et al.: *Equality under Pressure. Challenges for the Scandinavian Model of Distribution.*

CHAPTER 4

Immigration in Italy: Subverting the Logic of Welfare Reform?

Giuseppe Sciortino

In international policy circles and public opinion alike, immigration to Italy evokes images of overcrowded boats crossing the Mediterranean, ferrying immigrants bound for a life of makeshift camps and odd jobs. It is usually taken for granted that Italian migration policies are largely ineffective, exploitative and occasionally cruel.[1]

As with most stereotypes, there lies within this a kernel of truth. Boats do indeed cross the Mediterranean in perilous, and often fatal, journeys. Italy has a sizeable irregular foreign population, currently estimated at around half a million. Makeshift camps and vagrant sites exist in several locations, particularly in the south and during the labour-intensive phases of agricultural activities.[2] The endless political conflict that surrounds immigration policy is ripe with populist frenzy, xenophobic statements and merely symbolic measures.

To rely on stereotypes, however, is a risky habit. Doxa is not necessarily episteme. The prevailing vision may appear self-evident but it is actually complacent, and forms a serious obstacle to the development of an adequate analysis of the Italian case, additionally hindering the broader understanding of European trends.

The fact is that the elements highlighted by these stereotypes make for compelling news stories, but are far from being the most structurally relevant, and are also increasingly inaccurate. Most irregular migrants in Italy, as in any other European country, are not clandestine arrivals but have overstayed their legitimate entrance visas. In the last decade, illegal border crossing has become difficult, as demonstrated by the diminishing number of arrivals and the steep increase in prices requested by smugglers.[3] The size of Italy's irregular foreign population does not seem to be extraordinary when set against other European countries. The many amnesties of the past (and the recent downturn in the economy) have strongly reduced the size of the irregular resident foreign population, and the eastern enlargement has regularised overnight a large number of illegitimate residents, providing a large supply of foreign workers with a valid legal status.[4]

The problems raised by a reliance on stereotypes do not end with simple inaccuracies and errors. As will be seen in the following pages, the most pressing aspect of the current obsession over border sovereignty and internal public order lies instead in the fact that it obscures the immigration dynamics that are the most significant for Italy's economy and society. Immigration to Italy, largely consisting of labour migration, plays an ever more crucial role in the country's limited welfare model. Immigrants supplant the role played by the state in less conservative welfare regimes, providing the services necessary to the country's ageing population and helping to keep Italy's stagnating economy afloat. Only when this context is taken into account does it become possible to understand important features of Italian immigration policy, including its stable commitment, despite recurrent failures, to pursue an active labour immigration policy for foreign, low-skilled workers. This perspective on the way in which Italian immigration is shaped by the demand for services from citizens also highlights the relative unimportance of border management as a policy shortcoming, in comparison to the lack of integration between immigration policy, economic policy and a consistent strategy of welfare reform.

Despite the Downturn: Italy's Enduring Labour Immigration

There is no doubt that Italy has experienced a massive immigration flow in recent years. That 4,500,317 foreign citizens were registered as regularised residents at the end of 2010, making up 7.5 per cent of the population, may not seem particularly impressive. But the number of immigrants has more than tripled in less than a decade. Between 2005 and 2010, the immigrant population in Italy has increased, on average, by 400,000 individuals each year, the vast majority of whom are new arrivals. Italy has also been disproportionately impacted by the eastern enlargement of the EU. With more than one quarter of the current foreign population made up of EU citizens – entitled to a consistent set of legal, social and (limited) political rights – the typical migratory scenario has changed drastically in just a few years.[5]

The recent economic downturn has curtailed the growth of the foreign population, but has not significantly modified the trend. In 2009, when Italy recorded one of the worst GDP performances of the last thirty years, the foreign population actually increased by a greater amount than it had in the previous year. Even if the macroeconomic outlook is rather gloomy, the attractiveness of Italy as a migratory destination remains strong. In February 2011, when the website designed to receive the applications for the 98,000 work visas allotted by the government for non-EU workers was activated, nearly 400,000 applications were filed in less than two days, half of them within the first 30 minutes.

In many ways, immigration to Italy is very similar to the classical European labour migration of the 1960s in the Northern European countries. It is, in fact, overwhelmingly made up of foreign *workers*, entering to fill shortages in low-skilled labour sectors, later bringing their families (the only concession to the postmodern condition being that the typical migrant is now often a woman). The foreign population in Italy is characterised by a high labour-market participation rate. According to Italy's *Labour Force Survey* results in 2009, 76 per cent of male foreign workers were gainfully employed during the year (compared to an EU average of 68 per cent). The foreign women's participation rate, while markedly lower at 63 per cent, was still higher than the EU average of 60 per cent. Across the EU countries surveyed, only the United Kingdom showed similar (or slightly higher) rates. More remarkably, the percentages of foreign residents in gainful employment was significantly higher than those of Italian citizens in the same cohorts, whose employment rates were respectively 67 per cent (for men) and 45 per cent (for women).

Another strong similarity to the classical European labour migration of bygone days is reflected in the fact that current migratory flows largely consist of manual labourers. Seventy-six per cent of foreign workers are employed in low-skilled occupations (compared to 32 per cent of natives). Their presence has become quite sizeable in the sector of unskilled occupations, where they account for nearly 33 per cent of the labour force.

Why hasn't the economic downturn abated the demand for foreign workers? To understand recent developments, it is necessary to place them in the broader context of the Italian economy's evolving structure. Over the last decade, long before the downturn, Italy's economic performance has been comparatively dismal, with a sharp decrease in the growth of the real GDP resulting largely from the stagnant level of labour productivity.[6] A large portion of the Italian economy is concentrated in construction and other labour-intensive services which, stacked against globalised competitors, are characterised by high numbers of small companies and businesses that cannot produce similar economies of scale or use the factors of production as efficiently. Other than resorting to tax evasion, their survival and profitability has come to rely on lowering labour costs and drawing increasingly on short-term, discretionary contracts. These are the sectors that have been among the main beneficiaries of the labour-market reforms carried out since 2000, which have been primarily centred on protecting labour-market 'insiders' – the baby boomer cohort – while at the same time implementing strong deregulation designed to increase flexibility for marginal workers.[7] Traditionally export-oriented sectors such as manufacturing have by contrast fared badly, for reasons which include inadequate size, low expenditures in R&D, difficulties in leaving their mature niches and poor infrastructural support. Employees in these sectors – being exactly the kind of workers the Italian welfare state was originally designed to protect – have enjoyed a relatively high level of protection from the traditional risks of the industrial working class. But they have paid for such protection with severe constraints on wages matched by comparatively high levels of taxation. Wage moderation notwithstanding, the lack of growth in productivity has given Italy one of the highest costs of labour per product unit, among Western European countries. In all sectors, a vicious circle of sluggish product competitiveness and labour deskilling has become increasingly evident.

These dynamics have resulted in the emergence of a strong demand for unskilled, cheap labour. During the last decade, the absolute number of employed individuals has markedly increased, and (before the crisis) the number of jobseekers had reached a historical low. The number of low-skilled, flexible jobs has been so high that even the underground economy – a traditional feature of the Italian economy – has shrunk.[8] The proliferation of such low-skilled, poorly paid and highly flexible jobs has, however, left a dearth of employment which matches the expectations of young Italians. Though the education revolution in Italy came late and remains incomplete, its effects are increasingly at odds with an economy that is structurally unable to provide the medium- and high-skilled jobs new entrants to the labour market seek. This explains why native jobseekers are nearly always young people looking for their first jobs. This demographic usually live with their parents, meaning many of them are able to wait for 'proper' employment. The past two decades have, therefore, left Italy with a strong dual labour market, combining a large supply of potential workers for a limited number of middle- and high-skilled jobs, with growing demand for low-skilled and unskilled workers where fewer exist.

Italian immigration dynamics have always been tightly intertwined with the growing demand for low-skilled, low-paying jobs. Seen in this context, the (often maligned) Italian habit of enacting frequent amnesty programmes for the irregular resident population appears quite effective. They have transferred a large number of immigrants from the shadow economy to the formal, low-skilled labour sector, where they were badly needed.[9]

The economic downturn seems to have strengthened and further accelerated this dynamic within the Italian labour market. The crisis has hit the middle-skilled and high-skilled strata, where foreign workers are underrepresented, with particular force. At the same time, it has triggered a compression of labour costs, which has translated, in turn, into an enduring demand for cheap, foreign labour. The best example of this dynamic is provided by the construction sector, which currently employs 17 per cent of the foreign workforce (nearly exclusively males). Since 2009, the downturn has led to an intense, and still incomplete, restructuring of the sector. This has not involved, however, the consolidation of firms into larger units able to operate in more complex markets, but rather their further fragmentation. There has been both a sharp decrease in the number of skilled and semi-skilled jobs (largely the province of native workers) and a sharp increase in low-skilled jobs, a large percentage of which has been filled by foreign workers.

Though the economic downturn has had only a mild impact on the employment rate of immigrants, it has had significant consequences for the quality of their jobs and their living standards. Foreigners are three times more likely than natives to be underemployed, and their career chances do not improve with immigration seniority. The income gap between natives and immigrants has widened and the percentage of working poor has increased.[10] The traditional dualism of the Italian labour market, in short, is becoming not only sharper but also increasingly polarised in 'ethnic' terms.

Immigration as a Pillar of the Welfare State

The particular dynamics of labour markets are deeply intertwined with the welfare regimes of their respective European countries. The Italian welfare state is strongly worker-oriented, centred on the male breadwinner model and tailored to provide services primarily through social insurance, which is contingent upon previous work performance. In principle, this model should be neutral in its approach to both natives and immigrants, as all its benefits are by definition open to all members of salaried occupations. A specific feature of the Italian welfare state, however, makes immigrants de facto net contributors: Italian social expenditure is largely focused on servicing pensions, both for retirees and survivors (Italy spends roughly twice as much as the OECD average on pensions). The main reason foreign workers contribute much more than they receive from pension funds is demographic. Among the resident foreign population, there are eight adults of working age out of any ten foreign residents, with the remaining two usually being minors. In principle, this difference should disappear in the long run, with the ageing of current immigrant workers, but in reality, they will never attain the same privileges. In 1996, when it had become clear that the Italian pension system – based on pay-as-you-go defined benefit principles – was no longer sustainable, it was reformed by switching to a defined-contribution system. To protect baby-boomer insiders, however, the transition was arranged in a way that kept the benefits of the previous system for those already within it largely intact, while the new – and much less generous – system was to be applied to all new entrants. As the vast majority of foreign workers arrived after 1995, they – together with Italians born after 1960 – are contributing both to the pensions of those (nearly all natives) who retired under the old system and to their own (paltrier) pensions. This situation provides further incentive for the Italian state to regularise as many employed immigrants as possible.

The weight of pension expenditures on the budget, as well as the pressing need to service Italy's outstanding national debt (118 per cent of the GDP in 2010), points to the fact that many other kind of welfare programmes are non-existent or heavily underfunded, leaving new problematic social configurations (including those typical of a large-scale immigration flows) lacking appropriate support.[11] There are no systematic income support programmes for those who have never worked or for the long-term unemployed, and the Italian state provides very few services in kind, from subsidised housing to education fellowships, or from childcare to job training schemes. In contrast to other European countries, immigrants are very unlikely to become welfare burdens, however hard they try.

At the same time, it is possible to argue that immigration has become one of the main pillars of the welfare regime.[12] The Italian Republic, like other conservative-style welfare states in Europe, entrusts their main welfare tasks to households, supporting them through monetary transfers rather than through the direct provision of services. Italian households consequently operate as general contractors, integrating the services they may self-produce with the little services in kind they can acquire from public bodies and the services they acquire on the market. Like any general contractor, they face constantly a *make-or-buy* choice. The Italian system has some advantages, as demonstrated by the fact that only 1.5 per cent of elderly Italians live in residential institutions, one of the lowest percentages of all OECD countries.[13] But it also has structural consequences, including a very low female labour participation rate and, more indirectly, delayed and low fertility, as the cost of having children becomes more significant.

Yet it has become increasingly difficult for Italian households to self-produce welfare services in the recent decades. Living standards have improved. The number of dual-career households has increased, albeit slowly. Lower rates of fertility have produced smaller households. The ageing of the population has increased the number of households where the basic needs of one (or more) members cannot be met by household members alone, while the prevailing cultural view remains opposed to the idea of entrusting elderly persons to institutions (regardless of their actual or potential quality). These trends create a strong demand for services acquired outside of the household. As the supply of state-provided services has been stable or even shrinking, much of the demand has been directed toward the private market for personal services.

The main problem, however, is that purchasing personal and household services is not easy. The mechanism is part and parcel of what is known in the literature as *Baumol cost disease*.[14] Because the productivity of personal services cannot be increased easily through organisational and technical means, and the salaries of service workers may stay in line with what is considered a 'decent' wage, the necessary services will be too costly for many households. Wages will outpace productivity, thereby pricing the services out of the market. If, on the contrary, the salaries offered in the service sector follow its productivity, the jobs provided by this sector will be highly unappealing and avoided by all those who can do so. In both cases, the lack of an adequate supply of affordable services puts a serious strain on the relationship between the male breadwinner model, embedded in the conservative-style welfare regime and the realities of an ageing population and an increasing female labour participation rate. Immigration may thus be considered a creative adaptation to the challenge of preserving the established welfare regime in a changing social environment.

Since the early 1970s, immigrants have helped to ease the strain, providing market-based personal and household services to Italian households at affordable prices.[15] Once begun, the flow of domestic workers quickly reaches a self-perpetuating stage. Workers already active in the local labour market act as triggers for further waves of new arrivals, using their own reputations as guarantees for the reliability of new workers. In the beginning, the arrival of 'exotic' domestic workers was seen by opinion leaders and the high-brow press as a form of conspicuous waste, an epiphany of the status anxiety of the Italian upper (and increasingly middle) classes. For a considerable time, this widespread assumption that the migration of domestic workers was a 'luxury' requested by spoiled households contributed to the lack of policy attention to the phenomenon. The foreign housekeeper – nearly always portrayed as a scantily clad and naïve black or Asian woman – provided the fodder for Italian TV comedies, comic novels and jokes.[16] Only at the end of the 1990s, when the migratory flows from Eastern Europe had enlarged the labour supply,[17] was it acknowledged that a substantial number of foreign domestic workers were actually performing care work, primarily for the large elderly population.

The importance of the migratory dimension of the domestic services market is easy to document. It is the only sector of the Italian economy which is largely dominated by foreign workers: for each native employed in this sector, there are three foreign workers.[18] It is the sector that absorbs 40 per cent of all female foreign workers and one fifth of the overall foreign employment. The demands of care work, moreover, are structural rather than cyclical. Half of the jobs for foreign workers since the economic downturn have been in this sector.

The demand for domestic services is also among the main preconditions for large-scale irregular migration flows. Live-in care work, the usual entry job in this sector, provides food and housing as in addition to a salary and, because it takes place within private homes, effectively shields the migrant (and the employer) from all kinds of controls. It is not a coincidence that while the presence of irregular immigrants in other sectors has decreased over time, the opposite has occurred in the domestic service sector. It currently provides a little less than half of all the jobs available to irregular migrants.[19] As I elaborate in the following section, the growing importance of foreign domestic work as a pillar of the welfare regime has increasingly shaped the structure of Italian immigration policy.

The Dismal Fate of the Italian Active Labour Migration Policy

Italy is one of the very few Western European countries that has always acknowledged the need for foreign workers,[20] making an effort to implement an active labour immigration policy. Between 2006 and 2008, besides lifting the restrictions for citizens of the new EU member states, the Italian state had made available more than 700,000 additional long-term entry slots for non-EU foreign workers. From 2008 to 2010, despite the economic downturn, 250,000 long-term entry slots for non-EU workers were still provided.

Such policies, however, have largely failed in preventing the development of large-scale irregular flows, acting instead as a tool for the quick regularisation of migrants 'from within'. They have also quickly abandoned the promotion of an *immigration choisie*, restricting themselves to the management of the labour demand within the domestic services sector. Both outcomes are partially linked to some peculiarities of the Italian case. But they are also contingent upon the difficulties that *any* active policy would encounter when applied to the labour demand of a low-growth economy.

The basic assumption of Italian labour migration policy is that the encounter between foreign labour supply and demand has to occur before immigration begins. Employers must file a request for a specific worker while he or she is still abroad. The state authorises such requests if they are compatible with the so-called *carrying capacity* of the country, a notion that may be roughly interpreted as the volume of new entries being compatible with the available supply of jobs, housing and social services.[21] The main policy tool is the yearly decree that establishes the contingent of new work visas and sets the criteria for their allocation.

For approximately two decades, however, the goal of planning for the flows of foreign labour has proved elusive. Previously, planning was largely ritual, as the main source of legal foreign labour was provided by periodic amnesties.[22] When the new policy was actually implemented in the late 1990s, there was already in the country a generalised expectation, shared by employers and immigrants alike, that hiring an irregular immigrant and waiting for the next amnesty was the easiest and cheapest option.

Since 1998, the size of the established contingents of immigrants has become noticeable and has been accompanied by administrative efforts to make the policy work. Its impacts, however, have always been largely disconnected from the intended economic goal, for reasons both internal to the policy process and to the ways in which various social actors have reacted to it.

As an internal process, the main difficulty of utilising the yearly decree consistently and in tandem with a policy of labour-market reform has been the prioritisation of control measures over integration measures. One of the main reasons that Italy began seriously promoting an active labour immigration policy was the need to 'make a deal' with the main sending and transit countries, such as Albania, Tunisia and Morocco. Since 1998, Italy has reserved a large proportion of the entry slots for citizens of these countries in exchange for their collaboration in emigration control and readmission of their deported citizens. This exchange has been relatively effective, contributing to diminishing rates of clandestine immigration and higher rates of deportations.[23] But it has also had the consequence of making a large part of the labour contingent unavailable for skill-based criteria.

A second important difficulty is related to the neo-corporatist framework, with involvement of trade associations and trade unions, within which the planning process takes place. The actors involved are representatives of mature, and comparatively large-scale, industrial sectors, which are absorbing only a small percentage of incoming foreign labour. The employers actually using the most foreign labour – small farms, small businesses and households – are not usually members of organised interest bodies and are thus excluded from the game.

Another problem lies in the fact that while amnesties may always be presented as remedial actions for previous governments' mistakes, the creation of a yearly migrant contingent makes governments appear to actually desire further immigration, thus providing a weapon for all kinds of populist movements. Unsurprisingly, political considerations are usually stronger than econometric evidence.

The most fateful factor, however, is related not to the policy process, but rather to the radical mismatch that has emerged between the *conceptual* design of immigration policy and the actual dynamics of labour markets.

Italian labour migration policy presupposes an ordered world of treaties between states, a restricted number of employers who are able to plan their demand for labour over the medium term, governed by neocorporatist committees able to police their constituencies and negotiate realistic options. As I have shown in the section headed 'Immigration as a Pillar of the Welfare State,' immigration to Italy is embedded in a strikingly different reality. Although foreign workers have been able to join the industrial working class, it has occurred primarily in small enterprises. Most of the current demand for foreign labour originates in labour-intensive agriculture, in small firms active in the service sector and in private households. Here, employers are rarely able to plan their labour demand in advance and very often – this is especially true with households – they act under the pressure of sudden opportunities and constraints. For them, the very idea of hiring someone who is not personally known to them is uncanny. Because formal credentials and certification by public bodies are useless, they look for workers that can be tested directly and employed on the spot, perhaps after having been recommended by someone well known, usually another trusted worker. According to the Italian *Labour Force Survey*, only 4 per cent of the foreign workers employed in Italy in 2008 had found their job through some kind of formal agency or job centre.[24]

Furthermore, an active immigration policy requires a certain degree of control over the labour market. No selective process for admitting newcomers will work if there is widespread tolerance of the irregular employment of those who are already in the country. In Italy, however, this is a Herculean task. Most employers, and large sectors of public opinion, do not regard the hiring of an undocumented migrant as a criminal action. Putting cases of serious abuse, violence or overexploitation aside, hiring migrants is often considered a gracious, sometimes even charitable, act. Public opinion strongly supports the deportation of foreign criminals, misfits and troublemakers, but such measures are nearly always considered too harsh for 'honest' irregular workers. Although heavier employer sanctions have been introduced, they have never been systematically implemented, both for the lack of an adequate administrative infrastructure and, above all, for the fear of the political backlash they would trigger in a country where currently approximately 17 per cent of the GDP is undeclared.

The difficulties in/while enacting an adequate planning programme in this context have thus evolved, over the last decade, into an implicit compromise that defines the yearly contingent as a recurring 'mini-amnesty', not even particularly disguised. A large number of foreign workers enter every year as tourists, become working tourists and overstay their visa, waiting for the next recruitment-from-abroad drive. Once their visas are granted, they return to their home country, pick up their visas at the Italian embassy and return to their workplace as 'newly-arrived' workers. As a way of managing the irregular population, this compromise has significant advantages, allowing for a trial period that fits the exigencies of employers and (not infrequently) workers. It also keeps the spell of irregularity in the biographies of most immigrants reasonably short. But it implies that Italian immigration policy, far from steering the flows, is actually steered *by* them.

Because the yearly decree has become a tool for filtering access to the legal labour market, it has quickly lost any potential to contribute to the labour-market reform. Attempts in 2001 through 2006 to provide incentives for high-skilled foreign workers resulted in an utter failure for lack of demand, and have consequently been silently abandoned. Since 2007, the yearly decrees have been increasingly targeted at sustaining the Italian welfare regime through the regularisation of domestic and care workers. The satisfaction of the strong labour demand of Italian households, who by now regard the availability of foreign care labour as a de facto welfare right, is both politically uncontroversial and structurally necessary. In 2006, 12 per cent of the contingent had been allocated to domestic and care workers. In 2008, apart from the country-based quotas, the entire contingent was reserved for domestic workers. In 2009, not wanting to appear as if it was promoting further immigration, the government did not issue the yearly decree, but introduced in its budget reform package a new amnesty, restricted only to irregular immigrants employed as housekeepers or care workers. In 2010, apart from the country-based quotas, the entire contingent was again reserved for care workers. Immigration policy is increasingly constrained by the externalities of the strained welfare regime.

Conclusions

Contrary to widespread stereotypes, immigration to Italy is not a tale of destitute, clandestine migrants bound to a life of deviance and marginality. It is largely a story of classical labour migration, oriented toward providing needed workers for the unskilled and low-skilled segment of the Italian economy. What differentiates the current immigration flows to Italy from the pre-1973 experiences of Northern European labour-importing countries is the framework of the political economy within which it takes place. Far from answering labour shortages created by high rates of economic growth, foreign workers in Italy are actually 'pulled' by the strong demand for flexible and cheap labour, originating in the workings of a low-growth, low-productivity, mature economy and the growing difficulties of sustaining a conservative-style welfare regime. In this context, the various rounds of immigration policy reforms have been relatively successful in curtailing clandestine migration and in keeping the size of the irregular immigrant population within manageable limits. But they have largely failed both to plan the flows of new workers and in their ambition to steer demographic dynamics toward a more sustainable nexus among population composition, economic development and welfare development. In this sense, Italy seems to provide a perfect cautionary tale of the long-term dangers embedded in the idea that changes in immigration patterns may be produced simply by manipulating immigration policy, without deeper consistent reforms in the structure of labour markets and welfare provision.

Notes

1. For an academic example, see Calavita, K. *Immigrants at the Margins: Law, Race, and Exclusion in Southern Europe.* Cambridge: Cambridge University Press, 2005.

2. Cole, E. J. and Booth, S. *Dirty Work: Immigrants in Domestic Service, Agriculture, and Prostitution in Sicily.* Lanham: Lexington Books, 2007; Lucht, H. *Darkness before Daybreak: African Migrants Living on the Margins in Southern Italy Today.* Berkeley: University of California Press, 2011.

3. The boats so often seen on television are nearly exclusively carrying refugees, whose entry is not a matter of ineffective border controls but of the legal protection guaranteed by the non-refoulement principle of international refugee laws. The wave of arrivals triggered by the Tunisian revolution and the Libyan crisis seems more a short-term emergency than a shift in this trend. And, if anything, it is surprising how small the migratory consequences of the Middle Eastern upheavals have been until now: after several months, the number of arrivals is only slightly higher than the number of Albanian refugees that arrived in Italy in a single day in August 1991. See Pastore, F., Monzini, P. et al. 'Schengen's Soft Underbelly? Irregular Migration and Human Smuggling Across Land and Sea Borders to Italy. *International Migration*, 44/4 (2006): 95–119.

4. For other attempts at estimating comparatively the size of irregular foreign population, see the results of the recent project *Clandestino: Counting the Uncountable* (http://clandestino.eliamep.gr/category/clandestino-database-on-irregular-migration). The best critical analyses and systematic comparisons available are provided by Colombo, A. *Fuori controllo? Realtà e miti dell'immigrazione in Italia.* Bologna: Il Mulino, 2011; and Blangiardo, G. and Rimoldi, S. 'Flussi ridotti e più disoccupazione'. *Libertà Civili*, 4/1 (2011): 115–27.

5. Vasileva, K. *Population and Social Conditions*. Eurostat Statistics in Focus, 34/2011. Brussels: Eurostat, 2011.

6. A systematic analysis of the relationships between migration flows and the dynamics of the Italian economic system before the downturn may be found in Reyneri, E. *Immigration in Italy: Trends and Perspectives*. IOM: Argo, 2007.

7. Barbieri, P. 'Italy: "No Country for Young Men (and Women)".' In H. Blossfeld, S. Buchholz, D. Hofacker and K. Kolb (eds) *Globalised Labour Markets and Social Inequality in Europe* (pp. 108–48). Basingstoke: Palgrave Macmillan, 2011.

8. Istituto nazionale di statistica. *La misura dell'economia sommersa*. Rome: Istat, 2010.

9. Carfagna, M.'Isommersie i sanati: Le regolarizzazioni degli immigrati in Italia. In A. Colombo and G. Sciortino (eds) *Stranieri in Italia: Assimilati ed esclusi*. Bologna: Il Mulino, 2002; Istituto nazionale di statistica. *Gli stranieri in Italia: Gli effetti dell'ultima regolarizzasione*. Rome: Istat, 2005; and Sciortino, G. *Fortunes and Miseries of Italian Labour Migration Policy*. Rome: CeSPI, 2009.

10. Istituto nazionale di statistica. Rapporto Annuale: *La situazione delpaese nel 2010*. Rome: Istat, 2011

11. Foreigners, moreover, are by definition excluded from what may be considered the largest indirect welfare programme in Italy: the provision of sinecures in public administration and state-controlled bodies. As they require Italian citizenship and state-recognised educational credentials, the presence of foreign workers in this sector is minimal or non-existent.

12. Sciortino, G. 'Immigration in a Mediterranean Welfare State: The Italian Experience in a Comparative Perspective'. *Journal of Comparative Policy Analysis*, 6/2 (2004): 111–28.

13. OECD. *Help Wanted? Providing and Paying for Long-Term Care*. Paris: OECD, 2011.

14. Baumol, W. 'The Macroeconomics of Unbalanced Growth'. *American Economic Review*, 57 (1967): 415–26; Baumol, W. J. and

Oates, W. E. 'The Cost Disease of the Personal Services and the Quality of Life'. *Skandinaviska Enskilda Banken Quarterly Review,* 2 (1972): 44–54.

15. Sarti, R. '"Noi abbiamo visto tante città, abbiamo un'altra cultura": Servizio domestico, migrazioni e identità di genere in Italia'. *POLIS* XVIII/1 (2004): 17–46; Andall, J. 'Catholic and State Constructions of Domestic Workers: The Case of Cape Verdean Women in Rome in the 1970s'. In K. Koser and H. Lutz (eds) *The New Migration in Europe: Social Constructions and Social Realities.* Basingstoke: Palgrave, 1998; Gallo, E. 'Siamo partite per diventare suore: Storie di vita delle donne Malayali in Italia'. In A. Colombo and G. Sciortino (eds) *Stranieri in Italia: Trent'anni dopo.* Bologna: Il Mulino, 2008.

16. Sciortino, G. and Colombo, A. 'The Flow and the Flood: Immigrants in the Italian Newspaper Discourse'. *Journal of Modern Italian Studies,* 9/1 (2004): 94–113.

17. Catanzaro, R. and Colombo, A. (eds) *Badanti e Co: Il lavoro domestico straniero in Italia.* Bologna: Il Mulino, 2009.

18. Istituto nazionale di statistica: *Rapporto Annuale: La situazione del paese nel 2010.*

19. Blangiardo, G. C. *La presenza straniera in lombardia.* Milan: Fondazione Ismu, 2011.

20. Ambrosini, M. *La Fatica Di Integrarsi: Immigrati E Lavoro in Italia.* Bologna: Il Mulino, 2001.

21. For a detailed description of the evolution of Italian immigration policies, see Zincone, G. 'The Making of Policies: Immigration and Immigrants in Italy'. *Journal of Ethnic and Migration Studies,* 32/3 (2006): 347–75; Einaudi, L. *Le politiche dell'immigrazione in Italia dall'unità a oggi.* Bari: Laterza, 2007; Sciortino: *Fortunes and Miseries of Italian Labour Migration Policy.*

22. Barbagli, M., Colombo, A. et al. (eds) *I sommersi e i sanati: Le regolarizzazioni degli immigrati.* Bologna: Il Mulino, 2004.

23. Ritaine, E. (ed.) *L'europe du sud face à l'immigration: Politique de l'etranger.* Paris: Presses Universitaires de France, 2005;

Cvajner, M. and Sciortino, G. 'Dal Mediterraneo al Baltico? Il cambiamento nei sistemi migratori Italiani'. In R. Catanzaro and G. Sciortino (eds) *La fatica di cambiare: Rapporto sulla società Italiana.* Bologna: Mulino, 2009.

24. Istituto nazionale di statistica. *L'integrazione nel lavoro degli stranieri e dei naturalizzati Italiani.* Rome: Istat, 2009.

Further Reading

Bonifazi, C. *L'immigrazione straniera in italia.* Bologna, Il Mulino, 2007.

CHAPTER 5

Responding to Employers: Skills, Shortages and Sensible Immigration Policy[1]

Martin Ruhs and Bridget Anderson

Introduction

Labour immigration policies throughout developed nations seek to address a key question: how to shape the admission of new migrants as workers, to suit the 'needs' of the domestic labour market and economy more generally. What these needs are, how they vary across sectors and occupations, and how they change during periods of economic growth and crisis are highly contested points of inquiry. There is significant controversy about what role migrants can, or should, play in meeting 'skills needs' and in reducing 'labour and skills shortages' in various sectors and occupations. Employers often claim, in particular but not exclusively during times of economic growth, that there is a 'need' for migrants to help fill labour and skills shortages and/or to do the jobs that, they allege, domestic workers will not or cannot do. Sceptics, including some trades unions, argue that in many cases these claims simply reflect a broad preference on the part of employers, for the recruitment of cheap and exploitable migrant workers in order to avoid higher wages and investment in the training and skills development of domestic workers. As unemployment rises, some argue, the economy's need for migrant workers declines. However, others point out that, within highly segmented labour markets and a differentiated economy, even times of economic downturn may require new migrant workers with particular qualities, and in some occupations, they may be critical to economic recovery.[2]

How should government evaluate and respond to employers' claims that migrants are needed to fill labour and skills shortages?

This chapter reviews some of the key issues and insights from existing research to address this central question, which is at the heart of labour immigration policy in all countries.

Shortages and Skills are Slippery Concepts that are Difficult to Define and Measure

Both 'shortages' and 'skills' are highly slippery concepts within the framework of political debate. There is no universally accepted definition of a labour or skills shortage and no one obvious 'optimal' policy response. The definition of a shortage that typically underpins employers' calls for migrants to help fill vacancies is that the demand for labour exceeds supply at the prevailing wages and employment conditions. Most media reports of 'labour and skills shortages' are based on surveys that ask employers about hard-to-fill jobs at current wages and employment conditions.

By contrast, a basic economic approach emphasises the role of the price mechanism in bringing equilibrium to markets that are characterised by excess demand or excess supply. In a simple textbook model of a competitive labour market, where demand and supply of labour are critically determined by the price of labour, most shortages are temporary and are eventually eliminated by rising wages that increase supply and reduce demand. Of course, in practice, labour markets do not always work as the simple textbook model suggests. Prices can be 'sticky', and whether or not and how quickly prices change crucially turns on the reasons for the labour shortages, which can include sudden increases in demand and/or inflexible supply. Nevertheless, the fundamental point of the economic approach remains that the existence and size of shortages critically depend on the price of labour.[3]

In a similar way, though a concept commonly used in academic, public and policy discourse, 'skills' remains a very vague term both conceptually and empirically. It can refer to a wide range of qualifications and competencies whose meaning in practice is not always clear. Some 'skills' are credentialised (e.g. National Vocational Qualifications, professional qualifications and apprenticeships), but what is and is not credentialised changes, and jobs can shift from being classified as 'low-skilled' to 'skilled' and vice versa without necessarily changing in their content. The limitation of formal qualifications as a measure of skills becomes most apparent when one considers 'soft' skills not captured through formal qualifications. They cover a broad range of competencies, transferable across occupations (rather than being specialised) from 'problem-solving' to 'team-working' and 'customer-handling' skills. Soft skills are often said to be particularly important in sectors where social relations with customers, clients and/or service users are important to the delivery and quality of the work. Certain 'skills' may be necessary to make sure the job is done in a way that contributes to a good service experience, rather than simply to complete the task. For example, the quality of care delivered in both health and social care sectors is affected by the soft skills of those providing care, with some service users actively expressing a preference for personal qualities over formal qualifications.

At the same time, 'skills' can also be used to refer to attributes and characteristics that are related to employer control over the workforce. A demand for soft skills can easily shade into a demand for employees with specific personal characteristics and behaviour.[4] Employers may find certain qualities and attitudes desirable because they suggest workers will be compliant, easy to discipline and cooperative. The fuzziness of 'skill' is further exacerbated by its application to demeanour, accent, style and even physical appearance.[5] As skills soften, these signifiers may assume greater importance for those occupations that are less regulated with respect to formal qualifications, and where employers consequently have greater discretion in recruitment.

Any discussion of 'skills shortages' needs to take into account the fact that employers play an important role in defining the competencies and attributes that are 'needed' to do particular jobs and in deciding the terms and conditions of the job. In some occupations, the skills and 'work ethic' demanded by employers are partly or largely a reflection of employer preference for a workforce over which they can exercise particular mechanisms of control and/or that is prepared to accept wages and employment conditions that do not attract a sufficient supply of domestic workers.

Why Some Employers Prefer Migrant Workers

In assessing employer demand for migrant workers, it is important to note that 'what employers want' (i.e. the skills, competencies and attributes required of employees) is critically influenced by what employers 'think they can get' from the available pools of labour.[6] The labour supply potentially available to employers (e.g. the unemployed, inactive, migrant workers, etc.) is highly diverse, has different expectations and is motivated by different factors to participate in the labour market. It is easy to see how, faced with a diverse pool of labour, employers can become increasingly 'picky' and demanding of the types of workers they 'need'. This raises the possibility that employers develop a preference for migrant workers (or particular types of migrant workers) over domestic workers, based on migrants' perceived superior characteristics and attributes.[7] In practice, this is reflected in the claim commonly voiced by employers that migrants have a superior 'work ethic' and 'attitude'. Claims of this sort are typically made for relatively new arrivals rather than for foreign-born individuals more generally. A number of factors may encourage employers to develop such a preference.

Some employers may prefer migrants because of their lower expectations about wages and employment conditions. Research suggests that employers are typically acutely aware of the economic and other trade-offs that new migrants are willing to make by tolerating wages and employment conditions that are poor by the standards of their host country, but higher than those prevailing in their countries of origin. This is not confined to the lowest-paying occupations and sectors in the labour market.[8] In the UK, employers in certain sectors such as agriculture openly acknowledge that most prospective British workers consider the wages and employment conditions they offer for low-skilled work to be unacceptable.

Second, some employers may develop a preference for migrants because of the characteristics and restrictions attached to their immigration status.[9] In most high-income countries, immigration policies are characterised by a multitude of status categories, such as work-permit holder, student, working-holiday maker, or dependent. Each status is associated with different rights and restrictions in and beyond the labour market. These restrictions, which cannot be imposed on citizens, may give rise to a specific demand for particular types of migrant workers. Some employers, especially those finding it difficult to retain workers in certain jobs, may, for example, prefer workers whose choice of employment is restricted, as is usually the case with recent arrivals and migrants on temporary visas. Immigration requirements can make it difficult for many migrants to change jobs. From the employer's perspective, the employment restrictions associated with particular types of immigration status may make migrants more 'suitable' and easier to retain in jobs that offer low wages and poor employment conditions.[10]

Third, because of their different frame of reference, new migrants may be prepared to accept jobs whose skill requirements fall significantly below their actual skill-levels and qualifications, creating 'high-quality workers for low-waged jobs', who may well be more attractive employees than the available British workforce. In some cases, employer demand for particular groups of migrant labour may reflect a demand for specified qualities or knowledge related to particular countries, including foreign language skills. In a globalised economy, both in high- and low-skilled sectors, employers may value the knowledge and contacts migrants bring from their countries of origin. Whether local workers can acquire similar skills specific to certain countries and regions, and can consequently provide particular products, trading links and services that are associated with these business areas, is more contested regarding applicants for low- and medium-skilled occupations, such as mid-level chefs, than for high-skilled occupations, such as financial services.

The perceived advantages of recruiting migrants can also include employers' preference for a 'self-regulating' and 'self-sustaining' labour supply.[11] Employers can use migrant networks to control and regulate the flow of labour. In the UK, recruitment through migrant networks is thought to be a very common practice among employers with a migrant workforce. Companies with a demand for a flexible workforce may make use of employment agencies to help find suitable workers.

Since employment agencies often have significant numbers of migrant workers on their books, they can play an important role in impacting on the national composition of the workforce.

Alternatives to Immigration

In theory, at an individual level, employers respond to perceived staff shortages in different ways. These include: (i) increasing wages and/or improving working conditions to attract more citizens who are inactive, unemployed or employed in other sectors. Alternatively, employers could increase the working hours and remit of the existing workforce, which may require a change in recruitment processes and greater investment in training and improving specific skills; (ii) changing the production process to make it less labour-intensive by, for example, increasing the capital and/or technology intensity; (iii) relocating to countries where labour costs are lower; (iv) switching to production (provision) of less labour-intensive commodities and services; and (v) employing migrant workers.

Of course, not all of these options will be available to all employers at all times. For example, most construction, health, social care and hospitality work cannot be off-shored. An employer's decision on how to respond to a perceived labour shortage will naturally depend in part on the relative cost of each of the feasible alternatives. If there is ready access to cheap migrant labour, employers are unlikely to consider the alternatives to immigration as a way of reducing staff shortages. Yet this choice, though in the interest of employers in the short term, will not necessarily lead to the best outcome for the sector or the national economy. There is clearly the danger that the recruitment of migrants to fill perceived labour and skills needs in the short run exacerbates shortages and thus entrenches the certain low-cost labour production systems, reliant on the intensive use of migrants, in the long run.

It is important to recognise that employers do not make their choices in a vacuum, but within the constraints of the wider institutional and regulatory framework that is, to a large extent, moulded by public policies. Public policies often incentivise – and can in some cases leave little choice for – employers in some sectors and occupations in responding to shortages through the employment of migrant workers. For example, the UK has long prided itself on its labour-market flexibility and its relatively low levels of labour regulation. Together with a range of policies on areas ranging from training to housing, this stance has contributed to creating a growing demand for migrant workers.

For example, in the construction sector, the difficulty of finding suitably skilled British workers is critically related to low levels of labour-market regulation and the absence of a comprehensive vocational education and training system.[12] The industry is highly fragmented, and reliant on temporary, project-based labour, informal recruitment and casual employment. These practices may have proven profitable in the short term, but they have eroded any incentive for employers to invest in long-term training. As a consequence, vocational education provisions are inadequate for the sector. By contrast, many other European states have well-developed training and apprenticeship programmes, producing workers with a wide range of transferable skills. It is often these workers who find themselves working in Britain on tasks such as groundwork or foundation-building, which is low-paid and has no formal training requirement, despite years of lobbying by contractors.

Social care is another sector in the UK in which public policies have created a growing demand for migrant workers.[13] Two thirds of care assistants in London are migrants. The shortage of social-care workers and care assistants exists largely as a result of low wages and poor working conditions. Most social care in the UK is publicly funded, but actually provided by the private sector and voluntary organisations. Constraints in local authority budgets have contributed to chronic underinvestment. Together with the structure of the care sector itself, this approach has resulted in a growing demand for low-waged, flexible workers. Simply cutting benefits, or reducing legal access to migrant workers without addressing the causes of British workers' reluctance to apply for jobs in this sector, will only put more pressure on an already creaking system.

Mind the Gap: Labour Immigration and Public Policy

Linking the admission of new migrant workers to labour and skills shortages requires critical analyses of precisely what constitutes the in-demand 'skills' and problematic 'shortages'. It is also important to consider how these crucial characteristics can be measured, in order to allow for a proper debate about whether immigration is the best response to the shortage. These requirements are challenging, but it is also important to recognise that a third question about alternative responses to shortages is an inherently normative issue that does not have a single 'right' answer. Deciding whether the optimal response to shortages should take the form of additional migrants, higher wages or some other option is a necessarily political issue, specific to the conditions of individual sectors, countries and circumstances, requiring the careful balancing of competing interests.

A second important implication of research for public and policy debates in this area is the recognition that employer demand for migrant labour is not simply a consequence of 'lax immigration controls'. It is also misleading to reduce the demand to easy slogans about 'exploitative employers', including: 'lazy locals won't do the work', or 'migrants are needed for economic recovery'. The rising demand for migrant workers in high-income countries often arises from a broad range of institutions, public policies and social relations. Curbing or at least slowing down the rate at which this reliance on migrants is growing – which is a policy goal of the current UK government – will not happen without fundamental changes to the policies and institutions that have created the circumstances producing the demand. In the UK, this includes greater labour-market regulation in certain sectors, more investment in education and training, better wages and conditions in some low-waged public sector jobs, boosts to job status and defined career paths and moves to tackle low-waged agency work. In the short-to-medium term, these changes are unlikely to occur within the context of the economic downturn and budget cuts – circumstances which are likely to do more to increase demand for migrants in low-waged sectors such as social care. In the long term, the key question is whether the UK is really able or willing to make the kinds of changes in wider public policies in exchange for fewer new migrants.

Notes

1. This chapter is based on the analysis in Ruhs, M. and Anderson B. (eds) *Who Needs Migrant Workers? Labour Shortages, Immigration and Public Policy.* Oxford: Oxford University Press (paperback published in 2012).

2. Finch, T., Latorre, M., Pollard, N. and Rutter, J. 'Shall We Stay or Shall We Go? Re-migration Trends among Britain's Immigrants'. Institute for Public Policy Research, London, 2009.

3. Migration Advisory Committee. 'Skilled, Shortage and Sensible, The First Shortage Occupation List for the UK and Scotland'. London: Home Office, 2008.

4. Payne, J. 'The Unbearable Lightness of Skill: The Changing Meaning of Skill in UK Policy Discourses and Some Implications for Education and Training'. *Journal of Education Policy*, 15/3 (2000): 353–69.

5. Warhurst, C. and Nickson, D. 'A New Labour Aristocracy? Aesthetic Labour and Routine Interactive Service'. *Work, Employment and Society*, 21/4 (2007): 785–98.

6. Ruhs and Anderson: *Who Needs Migrant Workers? Labour Shortages, Immigration and Public Policy.*

7. Waldinger, R. D. and Lichter, M. *How the Other Half Works: Immigration and the Social Organization of Labor.* Berkeley: University of California Press, 2003.

8. Anderson, B., Ruhs, M., Spencer, S. and Rogaly, B. 'Fair Enough? Central and East European Low Wage Migrants in Low Wage Employment in the UK'. Report written for the Joseph Rowntree Foundation, Centre on Policy, Migration and Society, University of Oxford, Oxford, 2006.

9. See for example Bloomekatz, R. 'Rethinking Immigration Status Discrimination and Exploitation in the Low-Wage Workplace'. *UCLA Law Review*, 54/6 (2007): 1963–2010.

10. Anderson, B. 'Migration, Immigration Controls and the Fashioning of Precarious Workers'. *Work, Employment and Society*, 24/2 (2010): 300–17.

11. Rodriguez, N. '"Workers Wanted": Employer Recruitment of Immigrant Labour'. *Work and Occupations*, 31/4 (2004): 453–73.

12. For more detailed discussion see Chan, P., Clarke, L. and Dainty, A. 'The Dynamics of Migrant Employment in Construction: Can Supply of Skilled Labour ever Match Demand?'. In M. Ruhs and B. Anderson (eds) *Who Needs Migrant Workers? Labour Shortages, Immigration and Public Policy*. Oxford: Oxford University Press, 2010.

13. Moriarty, J. 'Competing with Myths: Migrant Labour in Social Care'. In M. Ruhs and B. Anderson (eds) *Who Needs Migrant Workers? Labour Shortages, Immigration and Public Policy*. Oxford: Oxford University Press, 2010; Cangiano, A., Shutes, I., Spencer, S. and Leeson, G. 'Migrant Care Workers in Ageing Societies: Research Findings in the United Kingdom'. Centre on Migration, Policy and Society, University of Oxford, Oxford, 2009.

Further Reading

Migration Advisory Committee. 'Limits on Migration'. Home Office, London, 2010.

CHAPTER 6

European Employers and the Rediscovery of Labour Migration

Georg Menz

Introduction

Since the early 2000s, managed labour migration has undergone a remarkable renaissance in Europe. Notwithstanding a sizeable presence of the xenophobic Far Right, lacklustre support in public opinion polls and persistent unemployment, European governments have re-discovered the uses of labour migrant recruitment. The economic recession commencing in 2008 has not, it seems, had a dramatic impact on regulation yet, although immigration to countries experiencing severe downturns appears to have slowed somewhat.

This chapter assesses the role of non-state actors in lobbying governments and influencing the design of labour migration policies, with a particular focus on the work of employer associations. While other factors obviously may also play a role, notably the media, parliamentary institutions, the legacy of past regulatory policies and generally hostile public opinion, the role of interest groups is often either underspecified or relatively neglected in accounts of European migration policy design.[1] This may be due to a somewhat state-centric bias in the burgeoning literature on comparative European migration policies.[2] The excellent case studies that do examine such interest group activity focus on trade unions, arguing that unions prefer regulated labour migration to undocumented flows into the 'black' sector of the labour market.[3] Gary Freeman's important contributions emphasise the importance of employer associations and ethnic advocacy groups in shaping migration policies, though the empirical application is focused on the USA.[4]

When adopting a perspective influenced by recent advances in comparative political economy, it becomes clear that the interest positions held by employer associations reflect the national productive systems into which they are embedded. Therefore, the different characteristics that mark Europe's various models of politico-economic governance condition the demands respective employers make of national labour migration policies. Taking employer preferences seriously helps account for divergences in immigration policy preferences across different European countries. Employers do not univocally advocate the recruitment of identical profiles or numbers of economic migrants, nor are they all necessarily interested in simply a 'more liberal' immigration policy. The production strategies that underpin underlying different varieties of capitalism will lead employers to call for different types of labour migrants, while ideological coherence and successful appeals to the competition state agenda will lead to different degrees of success in shaping public policy.

Models of Capitalism, Employer Associations and European Migration Policies

European migration policies are rapidly changing. But who drives these changes? The paradox of liberalisation in the presence of a climate generally sceptical or even hostile towards immigration has previously been partially accounted for by the activities of liberal courts, while Freeman's pioneering work has emphasised the importance of client politics in liberal democracies – though principally the United States, where well-organised employer groups and ethnic advocacy groups combine efforts to press for liberal policies from which they benefit and whose costs are diffused.[5] Though compelling in its empirical application and rightfully applauded for its introduction of a political economy angle, Freeman's work has been criticised for not being applicable to the European context, where ethnic advocacy groups thus far play a limited role, and for neglecting how immigration is framed and thus perceived by actors.[6] Modifying Freeman's analysis somewhat, it is maintained that in the European context employers will not simply lobby for 'more liberal' policy, but rather the system of political economy in which they are embedded conditions the quality and quantity of labour migration advocated.

Recent advances in *comparative political economy* have stressed the resilience of national models or varieties of capitalism (VoC).[7] This highly influential, though also criticised, approach highlights the persistence of multiple equilibria in the institutional configuration of systems of political-economic governance, encompassing systems of industrial relations and labour-market regulation, vocational training and education, corporate governance and finance and intra-firm relationships.[8] It underlines fundamental differences between liberal and coordinated market economies (LMEs and CMEs), while recent contributions argue that many Southern European countries constitute amalgamated mixed market economies (MMEs) rather than separate statist models and that in Eastern Europe an even more transitory emerging market economy (EMEs) category has appeared.[9] As influential as the VoC debate has been in reshaping the subfield of comparative political economy, it has not thus far informed theoretical debates on migration, despite the obvious political-economic aspects of labour migration. Informed by VoC insights, it is argued that employer associations will seek to attract and recruit economic migrants that complement existing corporate strategies. These can be described as follows: gradual innovation and concentration on high value added production in CMEs, but radical innovation in LMEs. In terms of labour-market regulation and industrial relations, in CMEs co-determination, sectoral wage bargaining, sectoral wage parity, greater job security and longer tenure persist, despite serious erosion syndromes. This is not the case in LMEs, where significantly more pronounced wage and working condition differentiation exist and more macrolevel abjurations from wage settlements and deregulation in general prevail. Also, trade unions are legally constrained, and one generally finds shorter tenure and higher turnover in LME labour markets. Finally, regarding training and education systems, the situation in CMEs is characterised by sectorally portable skill sets, high skill and specialisation training strategies to sustain high value added export strategies. By contrast, individualised, company-specific skills, 'on the job training', and low general skill and education levels prevail in LMEs, although there are some important sectoral exceptions.

Employers will seek to lobby for legislation that ensures migrant profiles reflective of production strategies. Thus, in a CME such as Germany, we would expect an employer preference for highly skilled, top-tier labour migration. There is no appetite for low-skill migration. 'In contrast, in the UK, "deregulated" labour markets and the absence of labour as a countervailing force make a lower-cost, lower-price strategy, underpinning service-sector expansion more realistic.'[10] Thus, in an LME, employers are likely to advocate recruitment of highly skilled labour for *both* select niches with labour shortages and poorly paid sectors of the labour market that experience recruitment problems and high staff turnover. The service sector employs a higher percentage of the workforce, but this does not reflect a higher contribution to overall GDP, suggesting a sizeable low-waged, low-skill sector. In LMEs, there is generally more employer-specific and on-the-job training.[11]

Despite their heterogeneity and hybrid status, MMEs such as France and Italy have often-sizeable high-skill, high-wage clusters in the secondary sector. EMEs such as Poland, where CME-style coordination is very weak and underdeveloped, would appear to be slowly constructing these, but – setting them apart from southern and northwestern Europe – also still possess sizeable primary sectors.[12] In terms of the corporate strategies, the configuration of the labour markets, the state of industrial relations, and education and training therefore present a somewhat unwieldy hybrid. In terms of employers' labour recruitment strategies, this means that MME employers will be deeply divided between sectoral associations interested in highly skilled labour migrants and sectors that are more reliant on low-skilled employees who can be easily recruited domestically. Reflecting this internal division, one would expect only limited advocacy by employers for more liberalised labour migration. This is even more pronounced in EMEs, where the CME-style sectors of the economy are so small that migrant labour recruitment is of no real numerical and hence political interest to employers.

Managed Migration and Employer Preferences: The Politics of Advocating Liberalised Labour Migration Policy

Developments in four European countries are analysed here as representative cases of different constellations of political-economic governance, including the United Kingdom (LME), France (MME), Germany (CME) and Poland (EME). It is agued that *employer preferences are shaped by the system of political economy (or variety of capitalism) they are embedded in.*

France

For many years, French employers' interest in labour migration was limited.[13] French policymakers began exploring active labour migrant recruitment in the late 1990s. In 1998, an internal administrative circular had advised provincial governments to consider 'fast-tracking' (or at least treating with leniency) residency-permit applications from information technology experts; this spawned a 2001 governmental initiative to grant working and residency permits to a total of 4,000 information technology specialists.[14] Despite the restrictive Pasqua Laws being only a few years old, there were signs that the paradigm of zero (illegal) immigration was slowly being abandoned among the political Right. The 1998 Chèvenement Law permits the fast-track processing of residency and work permit applications by 'desirable' labour migrants. The number of permanent work permits issued fluctuated between 6,403 in 2000 and 8,920 in 2005.[15] This somewhat divided and reticent stance began to change. The employer association *Mouvement des entreprises en France* (MEDEF) itself remained reluctant to endorse in public active labour recruitment.[16] But the business-friendly thinktank Institute Montaigne began advocating the introduction of migration quotas and the active recruitment of highly skilled migrants in particular.[17] Its publications make the link between competitiveness and selective immigration very explicit, criticising that human right considerations have taken precedence to economic concerns in past French migration policy, while suggesting that an immediate doubling of migration flows, based on a 'sélection des candidates', would immediately address worrying labour shortages.[18]

While the very notion of quotas and actively managed and selected immigration remains highly controversial among the political Left, former president Nicolas Sarkozy – minister of the interior from May 2002 to March 2004 – warmed quickly to the notion of embracing 'actively managed, not encountered immigration policy', based on the principles of 'growth perspectives, labour-market needs and accommodation capacity'.[19] At the 2006 MEDEF summer school, Sarkozy repeatedly emphasised the benefits of 'chosen immigration' for 'those for whom we have work' rather than the 'tolerated' flows arriving through family reunion, the latter of which accounting for 70 per cent of all permanent immigration in 2005.[20] The 24 July 2006 so-called Sarkozy II Law obliged government to draw up a list of economic sectors experiencing labour shortages and facilitate economic migrant access. Most innovative, however, is the introduction of the *carte compétences et talents* for skilled migrants, motivated by the desire to raise the level of labour migrants and to abandon the previous principle of a general labour-market review as one condition for approving new work permits. MEDEF, which was informally consulted throughout the drafting process, enthusiastically supported the new direction chosen in labour migration. The internationally active companies were particularly vocal in supporting facilitated access to the best brains, but several sectoral associations experiencing labour-market shortages shared this enthusiasm.[21]

Germany

While German employers maintained an interest in the guestworker system even after the end to active recruitment in 1973, their position did not influence the political agenda, and by 1983 employer organisation Bundesvereinigung der Deutschen Arbeitgeberverbände (BDA) had given up its earlier lobbying. Behind the backdrop of rising unemployment, advocating new labour migration would not only have been difficult to defend politically, but also appeared unnecessary. However, by the late 1990s change was underway. Outspoken Bundesverband der Deutschen Industrie (BDI) president Hans-Olaf

Henkel called for liberalised legal labour migration in a general quest to render Germany's economy more dynamic and competitive. The BDA slowly embraced this stance. The employers were represented in two government expert commissions on immigration, and they harshly criticised the Christian Democrats' rejection of labour migration quotas.[22] BDA enthusiastically welcomed the 'new paradigmatic change' inherent in the hotly contested immigration draft bill, which was not implemented until 2005. Convinced of the necessity to 'compete for the best brains' and 'internationally mobile high flyers' to address 'labour-market shortages' and to ensure the continued 'competitiveness of Germany as place to do business', regulation concerning economic migration needs to be liberalised, permitting both temporary and long-term migration flows, with minimal discretion for local and regional administrative interventions.

Policymakers responded to these demands. In 2000, a temporary labour recruitment programme for 20,000 highly skilled migrants was launched, particularly in IT (the so-called 'green card' initiative). The next summer, an expert commission composed of academics, legal experts, the social partners and politicians from all parties was formed to deliberate on major reform of immigration legislation. The resulting 2005 'Law on the management and limitation of inward migration and the regulation of the residence and integration of EU citizens and foreigners' contained a cautious liberalisation of labour migration. Article 18 specifies that in processing an application for a work permit (henceforth linked to a residency permit), consideration should be given to the labour-market situation, the fight against unemployment and the exigencies of securing national competitiveness. The employer association had been consulted throughout the drafting of the bill.[23] Employers were particularly interested in highly skilled migrants, not least due to the positive experiences with the IT sector programme, and contributed to the demand for an annual migration quota, based on a points system.[24] Consistent lobbying led to the creation of migration channels for highly skilled, high-wage professionals in the new immigration bill – namely entrepreneurs investing at least one million euros and creating at least ten new jobs – and carefully delineated categories of highly skilled migrants were permitted access, including teachers, scientists and skilled managers earning in excess of 100,000 euros (all defined in Art. 19).

Following a meeting of ministers in Merseburg in August 2007, further business-friendly concessions were made effective as of November 2007, including facilitated access for CEE engineers, three-year work permits for foreign graduates of German universities and the creation of a working group within the Ministry of Labour and Education charged with developing 'a labour market-oriented man-agement of migration', including the examination of a points-based system measuring qualification levels, age and language skills.[25] Vice-chancellor and Minister of Labour Müntefering announced that there was no need for low-skill labour migration. The employers enthusiastically welcomed the liberalisation of access, emphasising labour shortages not only in engineering, but also in banking and business services, and continued their advocacy of the 'long overdue introduction' of such a points-based system, pointing to Britain as a possible model.[26]

The United Kingdom

British employers assume an active stance in advocating immigrants considered of economic utility, which covers both highly skilled and unskilled labour migrants.[27] The flexibility, additional skill base, of-ten superior training, educational standards, and soft skills such as higher motivation that are associated with economic migrants are all attractive factors leading British employers to embrace managed migration and lobby strongly in its favour. In mid-2005, CBI pres-ident Digby Jones stressed the advantage Britain enjoyed thanks to its flexible labour markets and pragmatic labour migration schemes. This position has been warmly received by the government; during an April 2004 speech at the CBI, Prime Minister Tony Blair argued that 'recognition of the benefits that controlled migration brings not just to the economy but to delivering the public and private services on which we rely' was needed.[28]

British employers assume an active stance in advocating immi-grants considered of economic utility, both in very highly skilled service sector jobs, especially in finance, law, health and natural science research, and in low-skill jobs in food processing, agriculture, gastronomy and construction.[29] Along with the union and certain NGOs, employer representatives are invited to the biannual 'user panel' planning sessions of the Immigration and Nationality Directorate in the Home Office. The CBI is also part of the employer taskforce group, which is responsible for providing policy suggestions to the Home Office's Border and Immigration Agency. Recommendations from this group have fed into the establishment of an Australian-style high-skill migration programme in February 2008 and the illegal working stakeholder group.[30] Within this taskforce group, along with a trade union delegate, major internationally oriented businesses such as Shell, Ernst & Young, Tesco, Citigroup and Goldman Sachs are represented as well as sectoral employer associations in engineering, hospitality and employment services, alongside NASSCOM, the Indian IT sector chamber of commerce. Both formal responses to government initiatives and informal avenues to the Home Office are fairly well received and the CBI has positioned itself well to influence governmental deliberations.[31]

British labour migration policy has undergone considerable changes in recent years. The 2001 Highly Skilled Migrants Programme (HSMP) first introduced an explicit points system, taking into consideration formal level of education, work experience, salary level, overall qualification and qualification of the spouse. Additional points were added for applicants in sectors with shortages – especially medicine – and, unlike the previous procedure, applicants themselves filed the application rather than their employer. Such a points system is also used to evaluate application by 'entrepreneurs' who plan to establish businesses. The HSMP was replaced in 2008 by a new points-based system with two tiers for 'highly skilled' and 'skilled' migrants respectively, also taking into account available funds and past UK residence or educational experience.[32]

The logic of the HSMP remains similar to that of the 2005 proposal's subtitle 'Making Migration Work for Britain', namely being based on a 'flexible, employer-led' logic.[33] Indeed, the document reiterates on 12 occasions that employers will be consulted or that the scheme is employer-led. Worth mentioning is also the establishment of the independent Migration Advisory Committee (MAC), consisting of independent academic economists and representatives of the Commission for Employment and Skills.

During the 2010 elections, the Conservative Party campaigned on a platform emphasising a more restrictive stance towards immigration. Despite internal misgivings within the new Cameron–Clegg coalition, the new government did cap the number of work permits and sought to police student visa recipients more closely, many of whom had worked in low-skill service jobs.

Poland

The relative importance of the primary sector in terms of employment levels is striking, despite the privatisation of the employment-intensive, state-owned collective farms. Tertiarisation has not progressed as quickly, a trend reflected in employment levels. High unemployment and a significant demographic cohort currently entering the labour market, coupled with limited welfare transfer payment mechanisms, mean that labour recruitment is largely domestically oriented, while labour immigration is a quantitatively limited phenomenon. Labour immigration is limited to highly skilled service-sector positions experiencing skill shortages, or to low-paid, temporary, flexible employees in agriculture under conditions that Polish employees are hesitant to accept.

The employer camp is organisationally divided and lacks organisational coherence, but shares a lacklustre attitude towards new instruments in labour migration.[34] It enthusiastically welcomed the legislative measures undertaken in 2004,[35] creating a new and simplified labour permit scheme. The legislative status quo meets all current labour needs, permitting labour immigration in highly skilled service sector positions and, given the absence of visa requirements for Ukrainians, paths to flexible if undocumented economic migration in the agricultural, construction and personal care sectors. Though work permit applications imply a bureaucratic process and significant employer initiative, including proof that no Polish citizen is available for the position, while the jobseeker him/herself needs to apply from abroad, this is still an improvement over the legislative status quo ante. Ministry of Economic Affairs and Labour data indicate that 46 per cent of all migrants are employed as managers or consultants, mostly from EU countries, Oceania and North America.[36] Most self-employed business owners, making up another 26 per cent of the total, come from Asian countries, including prominently Vietnam and Turkey. Russia and other former Soviet republics are prominently represented among both legal and illegal migrants. In 2004, 7,845 of the total 18,841 permanent residency holders in Poland stemmed from the EU15, 2,750 from Ukraine, another 2,181 from successor republic to the USSR and 3,563 from Asia. Though organisationally perhaps not best positioned to affect governmental policy, labour migration regulation meets employer interests and, though restrictive, permits the recruitment of high-skill service sector employees.

Previous legislation in the field of labour migration was more burdensome for employers. The number of work permits issued annually throughout the early 1990s hovered around 11,000 according to the Ministry of Interior, but this met employer needs at the time.[37] From the late 1990s onwards, larger companies and Polish branches of MNCs began to attract more Western high-skill migrants and communicated this development to the employer associations.[38] Partially in response, the 9 September 1997 Decree of the Ministry for Labour and Social Affairs specified exceptions to the work permit requirement for foreign employees and fine-tuned work permit procedures. In light of emerging short-term labour market shortages, the government looked favourably upon applications from its eastern neighbours, especially Ukraine, Russia and Belarus. Partially as a result of the flexibilisation, the number of work permits issued rose to 15,307 in 1997 and reached 21,487 in 2004, 74 per cent of which applied to key staff in multinational corporations and only 339 to unskilled workers.[39] Local discontent notwithstanding, the relevant 1997 Act on Aliens, which rendered deportation of illegally employed foreigners possible, was not applied rigorously, with labour inspections in 2003 unearthing only 2,700 cases of illegal employment of foreigners, despite estimates of up to 500,000 undocumented employees.[40] This undocumented pool of immigrants constitutes a flexible buffer that renders advocacy of regularised low-skill migration less pertinent, while relatively bureaucratic and costly procedures deter employers from work permit applications in such instances.

Conclusion

Employer associations have rediscovered labour migrants. But employers are selective in terms of the migrant profile they seek to attract; their preferences are conditioned by the systems of political economy in which they are embedded. In the view of organised business, ideal migrants should fit easily into existing production systems and complement corporate strategies.

Employers have been very active lobbyists, especially in the UK and Germany. Different varieties of capitalism condition employer preference. British employers have become more actively concerned with labour migration policy in the wake of the highly advanced tertiarisation of the economy and clearly apparent skill and labour shortages. Labour recruitment focuses on the service sector and seeks to compensate for deficiencies in domestic training institutions. Concerns over such shortages, especially in engineering, IT and finance, have resulted in employer advocacy of liberal provisions for individuals with such skills. By contrast, French employers have only recently discovered the benefits of labour migration, given that neither skills nor labour shortages were as readily apparent as in Germany or the UK. Recent French government activities suggest an embrace of actively managed labour migration policy aimed at highly skilled migrants, complementing existing high-skill sectors. German employers, especially those in the manufacturing sector, notably metal processing association *Gesamtmetall*, have been strongly supportive of highly skilled migration, complementing a high-skill, high-value-added production strategy. Polish employers have only very recently become active in interacting with government authorities with a view to liberalising labour migration. Cavalier enforcement of labour regulations regarding low-skill workers and much simplified procedures for highly skilled migrants facilitates economic migration and largely meets current demands of employers.

From Tallinn to Rome governments are designing schemes that will facilitate the inflow of the 'best brains', yet employers insist that these brains (or brawn) fit into existing systems of political economy. Their political activities have been successful in influencing regulatory outcomes.

Notes

1. Demo, A. 'Policy and Media in Immigration Studies'. *Rhetoric and Public Affairs*, 7/2 (2004): 215–29; Breunig, C. and Luedtke, A. 'What Motivates the Gatekeepers? Explaining Governing Parties Preferences on Immigration'. *Governance*, 21/1 (2008): 123–46; Hansen, R. 'Globalization, Embedded Realism, and Path Dependence: The Other Immigrants to Europe'. *Comparative Political Studies*, 35/3 (2002): 259–83; Lahav, G. *Immigration and Politics in the New Europe: Reinventing Borders*. Cambridge: Cambridge University Press, 2004.

2. Castles, S. and Kosack, G. *Immigrant Workers and Class*. Oxford: Oxford University Press, 1973; King, R. (ed.). *Mass migration in Europe: The Legacy and the Future*. London: Belhaven Press, 1993; Fassmann, H. and Münz, R. *European Migration in the Late Twentieth Century: Historical Patterns, Actual Trends and Social Implications*. Cheltenham: E. Elgar, 1994; Uçarer, E. M. and Puchala, D. J. *Immigration into Western Societies: Problems and Policies*. London: Pinter, 1997; Angenendt, S. *Asylum and Migration Policies in the European Union*. Berlin: Europa Union Verlag, 1999; Geddes, A. *Immigration and European Integration: Towards Fortress Europe?* Manchester: Manchester University Press, 2000; Geddes, A. *The Politics of Migration and Immigration in Europe*. London: Sage, 2003; Guiraudon, V. and Joppke, C. (eds) *Controlling a New Migration World*. London: Routledge, 2001; Cornelius, W., Martin, P. L. and Hollifield, J. F. (eds) *Controlling Immigration: A Global Perspective*. Stanford: Stanford University Press, 2004; Lahav, G. and Guiraudon, V. 'Actors and Venues in Immigration Control: Closing the Gap between Political Demands and Policy'. *West European Politics*, 29/2 (2006): 210–23; Messina, A. *The Logics and*

Politics of Post-WW II Migration to Western Europe. Cambridge: Cambridge University Press, 2007.

3. Haus, L. *Unions, Immigration, and Internationalization: New Challenges and Changing Coalitions in the United States and France.* Basingstoke: Palgrave Macmillan, 2002. Watts, J. R. *Immigration Policy and the Challenge of Globalization: Unions and Employers in Unlikely Alliance.* Ithaca: Cornell University Press, 2002; Penninx, R. and Roosblad, J. *Trade Unions, Immigration and Immigrants in Western Europe 1960–1993.* New York: Berghahn Books, 2000; Caviedes, A. 'Chipping Away at Fortress Europe: How Sectoral Flexibility Needs Shape Labor Migration Policy'. PhD Dissertation, University of Wisconsin, Madison, 2006.

4. Freeman, G. 'Modes of Immigration Politics in Liberal Democratic States'. *International Migration Review*, 19/4 (1995): 881–908; Freeman, G. 'Winners and Losers: Politics and the Costs and Benefits of Migration'. In A.Messina (ed.) *West European Immigration and Immigrant Policy in the New Century.* Westport: Praeger, 2002; Freeman, G. 'National Models, Policy Types and the Politics of Immigration in Liberal Democracies'. *West European Politics*, 29/2 (2006): 227–47.

5. Hollifield, J. *Immigrants, Markets and States: The Political Economy of Postwar Europe.* Cambridge, MA: Harvard University Press, 1992; Joppke, C. 'Why Liberal State Accept Unwanted Migration'. *World Politics*, 50/2 (1998): 266–93; Guiraudon, V. 'The Marshallian Tryptich Reordered: The Role of Courts and Bureaucracies in Furthering Migrants' Social Rights'. In M. Bommes and A. Geddes (eds) *Immigration and Welfare: Challenging the Borders of the Welfare State.* London: Routledge, 2000; Guiraudon, V. 'European Courts and Foreigners' Rights: A Comparative Study of Norms Diffusion'. *International Migration Review*, 34/4 (2001): 1088–125; Freeman: 'Modes of Immigration Politics in Liberal Democratic States', pp. 881–908; Freeman: *West European Immigration and Immigrant Policy in the New Century*; Freeman: 'National Models, Policy Types and the Politics of Immigration in Liberal Democracies', pp. 227–47.

6. Joppke, C. *Immigration and the Nation-State – The United States, Germany and Great Britain.* Oxford: Oxford University Press, 1999; but see also Freeman: 'National Models, Policy Types and the Politics of Immigration in Liberal Democracies', pp. 227–47; Statham, P. and Geddes, A. 'Elites and Organized Publics: Who Drives British Immigration Politics and in Which Direction?' *Western European Politics*, 29/2 (2006): 245–66.

7. Coates, D. *Models of Capitalism: Growth and Stagnation in the Modern Era.* Cambridge: Polity, 2000; Hall, P. and Soskice, D. (eds) *Varieties of Capitalism: The Institutional Foundations of Comparative Advantage.* Oxford: Oxford University Press, 2001; Amable, B. *The Diversity of Modern Capitalism.* Oxford: Oxford University Press, 2003; Hancké, B., Rhodes, M. and Thatcher, M. (eds) *Beyond Varieties of Capitalism.* Oxford: Oxford University Press, 2007

8. Coates, D. *Varieties of Capitalism, Varieties of Approaches.* Basingstoke: Palgrave Macmillan, 2005.

9. Hancké et al.: *Beyond Varieties of Capitalism*; Schmidt, V. *The Futures of European Capitalism.* Oxford: Oxford University Press, 2002; Amable: *The Diversity of Modern Capitalism.*

10. Hancké et al.: Beyond Varieties of Capitalism, pp. 32–3.

11. Cf. Thelen, K. *How Institutions Evolve: The Political Economy of Skills in Germany, Britain, the United States and Japan.* Cambridge: Cambridge University Press, 2004.

12. Molina, O. and Rhodes, M. 'The Political Economy of Adjustment in Mixed Market Economies: A Study of Spain and Italy'. In B. Hancké, M. Rhodes and M. Thatcher (eds) *Beyond Varieties of Capitalism*, Oxford: Oxford University Press, 2007, pp. 224–9; Mykhnenko, V. 'Poland and Ukraine: Institutional Structures and Economic Performance', In D. Lane and M. Myant (eds) *Varieties of Capitalism in Post-Communist Countries* (pp. 124–45). Basingstoke: Palgrave Macmillan, 2007.

13. Watts: *Immigration Policy and the Challenge of Globalization: Unions and Employers in Unlikely Alliance.*

14. Circulaire DPM/dm2-3/98/767 du 28 décembre 1998; see also Morice 2000.
15. Régnard, C. 'Immigration et presence étrangère en France 2005: Rapport annuel de la direction de la population et des migrations'. Paris: Ministère de l'emploi, de la cohesion sociale et du logement, 2006.
16. Correspondence with the author, March 2006.
17. *Le Point*, 7 May 2002, *Le Figaro*, 15 February 2006.
18. Institut Montaigne. 'Compétitivité et vieillissement'. Paris: Institut Montaigne, 2003:192.
19. *Le Monde*, 8 February FR-GOV-1 interview with senior official at French Ministry of Interior Affairs, Paris.
20. MEDEF. 'Intervention de Nicolas Sarkozy'. Speech at the MEDEF Summer School, 31 August 2006. Paris: MEDEF, 2006; Régnard: 'Immigration et presence étrangère en France 2005'.
21. FR-GOV-2 interview with senior official at French Ministry of Interior Affairs, Paris.
22. *Manager Magazin*, 16 October 2000.
23. DE-BUS-1 interview with official at employer association BDA, Berlin; DE-GOV-1 interview with senior official at German Ministry of Interior Affairs, Berlin.
24. DE-BUS-1 interview with official at employer association BDA, Berlin.
25. *Berliner Zeitung*, 6 and 25 August 2007.
26. BDA. 'Newsletter: Diskussion um Fachkräftemangel gewinnt an Dynamik'. Berlin: BDA, 2007; BDA. 'Arbeitgeberpräsident Dr. Dieter Hundt: Einführung des Punktesystems ist ein längst überfälliger Schritt'. Press Release 46/2007. Berlin: BDA, 2007; BDA. 'Arbeitgeber begrüßen Beschluss des Bundeskabinetts zu kurzfristigen Maßnahmen gegen Fachkräftemangel'. Press Release 67/2007. Berlin: BDA, 2007; BDA. 'Arbeitgeberpräsident Dr. Dieter Hundt: Gezielte Zuwanderung ja, undurchdachte europäische Gesetzgebung nein!' Press Release 105/2007. Berlin: BDA, 2007.

27. UK-BUS-1 interview with official at employer association CBI, London.

28. Geddes, A. 'United Kingdom'. In J. Niessen and Y. Schibel (eds) *Immigrationas a Labour Market Strategy – European and North American Perspectives.* Brussels: MPG, 2005.

29. UK-BUS-1 interview with official at employer association CBI, London.

30. UK-BUS-1 interview with official at employer association CBI, London.

31. UK-GOV-1 interview with official at UK Home Office [Ministry of Interior Affairs], Croydon/London.

32. *The Guardian,* 30 October 2007.

33. Home Office. *Controlling our Borders: Making Migration Work for Britain – Five Year Strategy for Asylum and Immigration.* London: Home Office, 2005.

34. PL-BUS-1 phone interview with official at employer association PKPP, Warsaw.

35. Dziennik Ustaw, No. 27 – item 236–239 of 11 March 2004 and the 20 April Act on the Promotion of Employment and Labour Market Institutions, Dzienne Ustaw 2004, No. 99, item 1001.

36. Korys, P. and Weinar, A. 'Poland'. In J. Noesse and Y. Schiebel (eds) *Immigration as a Labour Market Strategy – European and North American Perspectives.* Brussels: MPG, 2005.

37. PL-BUS-1 phone interview with official at employer association PKPP, Warsaw.

38. PL-BUS-1 phone interview with official at employer association PKPP, Warsaw.

39. Kicinger, A. 'Between Polish Interests and the EU Influence – Polish Migration Policy Development 1989–2004'. CEFMR Working paper 9/2005. Warsaw: Central European Forum for Migration Research, 2005.

40. Interview PL-UNI-2; Kicinger: 'Between Polish Interests and the EU Influence – Polish Migration Policy Development 1989–2004'.

Further Reading

Books and Articles

BDA. 'Das Ausländerproblem: Die Grundauffassung der Arbeitgeber'. Cologne: BDA, 10 March 1983.

BDA. 'Stellungnahme zum Zuwanderungsgesetz'. Berlin: BDA, 16 January 2002.

Bleich, E. 'Review Article: Immigration and Integration Studies in Western Europe and the United States'. *World Politics*, 60 (2008): 509–38.

Commission for Racial Equality [CRE]. 'Capital can't afford racism'. *Catalyst Magazine*, Winter (2003–4).

Confederation of British Industry [CBI]. 'Business Summaries: Immigration and Illegal Working'. London: CBI, 2006.

Ensor, J. and Shah, A. 'United Kingdom'. In J. Niessen, Y. Schibel and C. Thompson (eds) *Current Immigration Debates in Europe: A Publication of the European Migration Dialogue*. Brussels: MPG, 2005.

Faist, T. and Ette, A. (eds) *The Europeanization of National Policies and Politics of Immigration*. Basingstoke: Palgrave Macmillan, 2007.

Aldershot: *Implications*. Aldershot: E. Elgar

Green, S. *The Politics of Exclusion; Institutions and Immigration Policy in Contemporary Germany*. Manchester: Manchester University Press, 2004.

Guiraudon, V. 'Logiques et pratiques de l'Etat délégateur: les compagnies de transport dans le contrôle migratoire à distance'. *Cultures et conflits*, 45 (2002).

Hollifield, J. 'Immigration and the politics of rights: the French case in comparative perspective'. In M. Bommes and A. Geddes (eds) *Immigration and Welfare: Challenging the Borders of the Welfare State*. London: Routledge, 2000.

Institut Montaigne. 'Mondalisation: Réconcilier la France avec la compétitivité'. Paris: Institut Montaigne, 2006.

Joppke, C. *Immigration and the Nation-State – The United States, Germany and Great Britain*. Oxford: Oxford University Press, 1999.

Kelly, R., Morrell, G. and Sriskandarajah, D. *Migration and Health in the UK: An IPPR Factfile*. London: IPPR, 2005.

King, R. (ed.). *Mass migration in Europe: the Legacy and the Future.* London: Belhaven Press, 1993.

Kretzschmar, C. 'Immigration as a Labour Market Strategy: France'. In J. Niessen and Y. Schibel (eds) *Immigration as a Labour Market Strategy – European and North American Perspectives.* Brussels: MPG, 2005.

Lavenex, S. 'The Europeanization of Refugee Policies: Normative Challenges and Institutional Legacies'. *Journal of Common Market Studies,* 39/5 (2001): 851–74.

Samers, M. 'Invisible Capitalism: Political Economy and the Regulation of Undocumented Immigration in France'. *Economy and Society,* 32/4 (2003): 555–83.

Sommer, M. and Hundt, D. *Miteinander statt Nebeneinander: Integration durch Fördern und Fordern.* Berlin: DGB and BDA, 2004.

Unabhängige Kommission. *Zuwanderung gestalten, Integration fördern,* Berlin: Unabhängige Kommission Zuwanderung, 2001.

Weil, P. *La France et ses étrangers: L'aventure d'une politique de l'immigration.* Paris: Calmann-Lévy, 1991.

Interviews

During 2004–7, an additional 30 interviews were conducted with representatives of trade unions, employer associations, national ministries of interior affairs and labour and social affairs in all four countries discussed here. A number of background interviews were also conducted with national labour market and immigration experts.

PL-GOV-1 interview with senior official at Polish Ministry of Interior Affairs, Warsaw.

PL-GOV-2 interview with senior official at Polish Office for Repatriation and Aliens, Warsaw.

PL-UNI-1 interview with senior trade union official at All-Polish Alliance of Trade Unions OPZZ, Warsaw.

CHAPTER 7

Long-Term Care and Migrant Labour in the UK

Isabel Shutes

The provision of care has long relied on both the unpaid labour of women in the family and the low-waged labour of women in the provision of care services. Yet, ageing populations in the UK and other Western countries present major challenges for public policy in the light of the growing need for long-term care provision for older people. Under current care patterns, it is estimated that expenditure on long-term care will have to nearly double from 1.4 per cent of GDP in 2007 to 2.7 per cent by 2032 to meet the increased demand for care and rising real unit costs of care. At the same time, the workforce caring for older people will need to increase by 79 per cent.[1]

Increasingly, migrant workers are being employed in the provision of care for older people in the UK and in other European countries, such as Austria, Ireland, Italy and Spain.[2] This has taken place in the context of the restructuring of systems of care for older people, involving shifting relations between the state, market, family and individual.[3] In Southern European countries, such as Italy and Spain, where the public provision of long-term care services has been more limited, migrant workers are increasingly employed in the household to care for older people.[4] However, in countries such as the UK, where the provision of long-term care services is more developed, migrant workers have also been increasingly recruited by providers of residential and home care services.

These developments point to the ways in which migrant labour has enabled Western welfare states to contain the costs of care.[5] They likewise focus attention on the intersections between state policies towards care and policies towards immigration, in framing the employment of migrant care workers in specific national contexts.[6] While differences in the provision of care for older people exist across

European countries, similarities are evident as regards the role of migrant labour within different models of care provision.[7]

This chapter examines the institutional context of the employment of migrant workers in the provision of long-term care for older people (aged 65 and over) in England/the UK,[8] exploring the intersections of state policies towards long-term care and policies towards immigration. It draws upon research carried out in England/the UK on the employment of migrant care workers (care assistants and nurses) by providers of residential and home care services for older people and by older people and their families. The chapter examines, first, the institutional context of care for older people in England in which the employment of migrant care workers is located, and, second, immigration policy and care work. It then examines the intersections of care and immigration policies with regard to the employment of migrant care workers by private sector providers of long-term care services and their employment in private households. It concludes by considering the implications of shifts in state policies towards long-term care and immigration for the care labour market and for migrant labour specifically.

Long-Term Care Services and Care Work

Different dimensions of the 'marketisation' and the 'privatisation' of care are evident in the restructuring of care for older people in European countries,[9] and have implications not only for the provision of care but for the structure of the care labour market.[10] First, these developments include the implementation of quasi-markets and the contracting out of service provision. This has shifted the balance of provision increasingly towards private (for-profit) or non-profit providers.[11] In England, while the state (through local authorities) is responsible for arranging care services for older people, including residential and home care provision, those services are mainly delivered by private sector providers. Eighty-one per cent of places in residential care homes are in the private sector, while the private sector now accounts for 77 per cent of care homes overall and for a similar proportion of home care agencies (76 per cent).[12] Indeed, the expansion of residential and home care provision in recent years has occurred mainly within the private sector.[13] The majority of providers are, overall, small- and medium-sized businesses, although there has been ongoing consolidation of ownership of residential care homes, particularly those with nursing facilities: more than half of nursing care homes are now operated by major companies.[14]

The contracting out of service provision has brought about a major shift in the employment of the long-term care workforce from the public to the private sector in England. The number of public sector (local authority) jobs in residential care was reduced by a third between 1999 and 2009 (from 66,971 to 45,110), and by 50 per cent in home care services (from 73,963 to 36,160).[15] Nearly half (49 per cent) of people working in direct care jobs are now employed in the private sector (547,300 workers), 23 per cent are in the non-profit sector and 14 per cent in the public sector.[16]

This shift in employment has implications for the conditions under which care labour is provided. Although care work has long been a low-waged sector of the labour market – associated with the gendered division of labour – wages are lowest and employment conditions less favourable for those employed in the private compared with the public and non-profit sectors.[17] Low wages, poor employment conditions, including unsocial hours, and a lack of career opportunities underpin major difficulties in the recruitment and retention of care workers over the past decade[18] – difficulties that affect the private sector to a greater extent. Vacancy rates in England in adult social care services are estimated to be double the average for all types of industrial, commercial and public employment.[19] Moreover, vacancies for care workers have more than doubled in recent years (July 2005 to December 2009).[20] Turnover in these jobs is also higher than in most other occupations: data for 2009 show that in England it is higher for care workers in the private sector (24.2 per cent) compared with the non-profit sector (17.6 per cent).[21]

Second, changes to the funding and purchasing of long-term care provision are also of significance. In England, estimates suggest that public funding contributes around half of total expenditure on long-term care.[22] Although there has been some increase in gross public expenditure on care for older people (aged 65 and over) since 2004–5 (an increase of 2 per cent in real terms between 2008–9 and 2009–10),[23] long-term care services for older people have been marked by long-standing problems of underfunding overall.[24] Indeed, inadequate funding for long-term care in England is a major policy concern given the rapidly growing demand for care.[25] Eligibility for publicly subsidised support has been increasingly targeted away from institutionalised forms of care and towards community-care provision and to older people with higher dependency needs.[26] This increased targeting of public support is associated with the role of private funding, including charges paid by individuals receiving public provision, extra support purchased by individuals in addition to public provision and support that is entirely privately funded.[27]

As regards the purchasing of care services, although local authorities are the main contractors of provision, there has been a shift towards the direct purchasing of care by individuals and their families through cash-for-care payments.[28] In England, 'Direct Payments' and 'Personal Budgets' provide those eligible for public support with the option of receiving a cash payment to directly purchase care services and to directly employ their care workers. There has been a rapid increase in older people receiving Direct Payments in England: from 537 in September 2001 to 20,610 in March 2008, though the numbers still remain relatively low as a proportion of older people receiving publicly subsidised support.[29]

In addition to the shift towards employment in the private sector, the direct purchasing of care by individuals through the use of Direct Payments has also brought about an expansion in the employment of care workers in private households. In England, 14 per cent of people working in direct care jobs are now employed by recipients of Direct Payments.[30] Older people who are paying for their care through other sources of funding, including those who are privately funding their care, are also directly employing care workers, though there is currently limited data on this group of employers and care workers.[31] Estimates suggest that 145,000 older people in England were funding their own domiciliary care to meet their personal care needs in 2006.[32]

A much higher number of people may be employing care workers for a wider range of support services.[33] The shift in the purchasing of care from the state to the individual has therefore also had implications for the privatisation of care work, positioning older people as potential employers of their care workers.

Immigration Policy and Care Work

Immigration controls, through the differentiation of rights and entitlements accorded to immigration status, affect employer demand for migrant workers. As discussed below (and examined in more detail elsewhere[34]), they thus shape positioning of migrant workers in care work.[35]

Prior to the introduction of the points-based immigration system in the UK in 2008, work permits could be obtained for the employment of migrant workers in particular occupations. These occupations included nurses and senior care workers in long-term care. Work permits data for health and medical services show an increase in work permits issued, including for nurses and senior care workers, from 1,774 in 1995 to 26,568 in 2004.[36] Data on the number of work permits issued for senior care workers specifically indicate an increase from 475 in 2001 to 5,720 in 2005, subsequently declining to 5 in 2008, when the points-based system replaced the work permits system.[37] However, the data refer to first applications only and therefore do not include the extension of work permits for senior care workers or applications for changes of employment. As part of an overall approach to labour migration that targeted 'higher skilled' and 'skilled' workers, the issuing of work permits for senior care workers became increasingly restrictive prior to the introduction of the points-based system according to the criteria for assessing the 'skilled' status of the work (including the required level of qualifications and wages attached to the job). The issuing of work permits was tied to the employer, who was responsible for applying to obtain and renew a work permit. Although work permit holders were entitled, in principle, to change employer, they were in effect dependent on the employer for their right to work and to remain in the UK.

In addition to routes of entry for labour migration, the enlargement of the European Union in 2004 also facilitated the employment of workers from the eight accession (A8) countries. Since 2004, data from the Worker Registration Scheme (WRS) (under which workers from the A8 countries were required to register) show that registrations of care assistants peaked at just under 2,000 registrations in the third quarter of 2005, subsequently declining to just above 500 registrations in the first quarter of 2009 – reflecting an overall decline in WRS registrations.[38] A range of other types of visa has also allowed for the employment of migrants in the UK, including in care work, such as students, domestic workers, working holiday makers and those entering through family reunion.[39] At the same time, the rights of non-EEA nationals to settlement in the UK (to obtain permanent residency and full rights to work and remain in the UK) have become increasingly restricted regarding the criteria for obtaining permanent residency, including length of stay.

Data and Methods

The sections below draw upon research carried out by the Centre on Migration, Policy and Society (COMPAS) at the University of Oxford on the employment of migrant care workers in the UK.[40]

Long-Term Care Providers

A postal survey was sent to a random sample of residential care homes ($N = 3800$) and a random sample of UK Homecare Association members (home care agencies) ($N = 500$) in 2008. The response rate was 12 per cent, providing a sample of 557 providers of care for older people overall. Eighty-two per cent of the sample was private providers, 15 per cent non-profit and 3 per cent public (local authority). Semi-structured telephone interviews were carried out with 30 providers, selected from the survey respondents (managers and owners of residential care homes and of home care agencies).[41]

Migrant Care Workers

In-depth interviews were carried out with 56 migrant care workers in England in 2007 (49 women and 7 men). The interviewees included

39 employees of private residential care homes and/or private home care agencies, 13 people who were employed directly by the older person for whom they cared, and 3 by the families of that person (1 respondent was employed by a local authority at the time of interview). All interviewees were foreign nationals, including EEA nationals (from Poland and other Eastern European countries) and non-EEA nationals (from countries such as the Philippines and Zimbabwe). Most had arrived in the UK between 1998 and 2007. Interviewees' immigration status varied at the time of interview, including those who had obtained permanent residency since coming to the UK, those who held work permits for senior care workers, domestic worker visas, student visas, asylum seekers and those who had overstayed entry visas.

Long-Term Care Services and Demand for Migrant Care Workers

In the context of the expansion of private providers of long-term care services, there has been increasing employment of migrant workers over the past decade. Labour Force Survey (LFS) data show that the proportion of foreign-born care workers in the UK more than doubled from 7 per cent in 2001 to 18 per cent in 2009.[42] The proportion of foreign born nurses increased from 13 per cent to 23 per cent over the same period.[43] As is the case for the UK-born care workforce, the majority of foreign-born workers are women (76 per cent), though less of a majority compared with UK-born care workers (among whom 87 per cent are women). While the private sector has become the main employer of care workers overall, migrant workers are overrepresented within the private sector: 79 per cent of foreign-born care workers (who entered the UK since 1998) are employed by a private sector organisation compared with just above half of UK-born care workers according to Labour Force Survey data.[44]

With regard to nationality and immigration status, recent data from the National Minimum Data Set for Social Care on the adult social care workforce in England show that 19 per cent of workers are non-UK citizens. However, there is significant regional variation: in London, just over half of these workers (51 per cent) are non-UK citizens, while the percentage is lower in other regions, such as the northeast of England.[45] Around a quarter (26 per cent) of workers in adult social care services who are non-UK citizens are EEA nationals. The majority (74 per cent) are non-EEA nationals who are subject to immigration controls, the main nationalities including the Philippines, India, Nigeria, Zimbabwe and South Africa.[46]

Among the providers surveyed in the COMPAS research, significant recruitment difficulties were reported. Half of the providers surveyed in the UK reported difficulties in recruiting UK-born care assistants, while 58 per cent reported difficulties in recruiting nurses. Providers identified low pay as the main reason for recruitment difficulties. The majority (87 per cent) agreed that UK-born workers can earn more in other jobs and (74 per cent) that UK-born workers demand higher wages than those paid in long-term care. Other reasons given for recruitment difficulties included the unwillingness among UK-born workers to work the shifts involved in care work (identified by 72 per cent of the providers). In follow-up interviews with providers, low levels of pay were attributed to the low levels of fees paid to providers contracted by local authorities.

While providers referred to difficulties in recruiting UK-born workers as the main reason for the recruitment of migrant workers, they also considered there to be advantages in employing migrant care workers. The majority of providers thought that migrant workers were willing to work all shifts (82 per cent) and had a 'good work ethic' (71 per cent). These perceived advantages of employing migrant care workers appear to be reflected in working patterns. According to LFS data, over 30 per cent of foreign-born care workers work more than 40 hours a week, compared with 18 per cent of UK-born care workers. Higher proportions of foreign-born care workers also do shift-work (74 per cent) compared with UK-born care workers (60 per cent).[47] Indeed, migrant care workers interviewed in the research, who were employed in care homes, indicated that their managers relied on them to work overtime and to work less favourable shifts compared with UK-born workers in order to address staffing gaps.

Particular categories of migrant workers, according to the terms and conditions of their immigration status, also provided a source of labour that employers were better able to retain compared with workers with rights of citizenship. As regards the difficulties of employing UK-born workers, 67 per cent of providers indicated that UK-born workers often leave the job. While EEA nationals from Eastern European countries were seen as 'hard working', they were also perceived by some providers as less reliable, in that, like workers who held UK citizenship or permanent residency, they did not face restrictions on their labour mobility. Care-related jobs could therefore be a 'stepping stone' into other types of work. Indeed, some care workers interviewed in the research who were EEA nationals themselves referred to entering care work because it was 'easy to find', while their intention was to move on to care-related jobs with better conditions or to other areas of work. By contrast, migrant workers who were employed on work permits for senior care workers were dependent on their employer for their work permit and, therefore, for the right to work and remain in the UK. Although they were, in principle, entitled to change employer, work permit holders interviewed in the research emphasised their fear of being unable to renew their work permit or apply for permanent residency or British citizenship in the future should they change jobs. Within this context, the conditions of legal status created a source of care labour less able to exit from an employer and more 'willing' to accept low wages and poor working conditions.[48]

At the same time, migrant care workers may also provide a more flexible source of labour due to the temporariness of their rights to employment. NMDS-SC data on the employment status of care workers show that while 15 per cent of care workers on permanent contracts are non-UK citizens, this percentage increases to 27 per cent of workers on temporary contracts, 41 per cent of agency staff and 62 per cent of students.[49] Migrant care workers interviewed in the research included those who held student visas doing temporary care work through home care and employment agencies. According to the terms and conditions of their visa, they faced restrictions on the number of hours that they could work and were not legally entitled to take up permanent, full-time work. These terms and conditions thus, in effect, enabled home care services to be provided at minimum labour costs.

Sometimes in home care I can have about 1 hour, 30 minutes, sometimes it can go for 6 hours a day. Sometimes you can work continuously, sometimes you can go for days without working...

(Care worker who held a student visa, working for a private home care agency)

The Employment of Migrant Care Workers in Private Households

Among the migrant care workers interviewed in this research, some were employed directly by older people or by their families in private households.[50] Most of these interviewees held domestic worker visas.[51] Migrant workers who held domestic worker visas were required, according to their visa, to be directly employed by members of the private households in which they worked. The terms and conditions of their legal status thus positioned them in privatised forms of care work within private households. Their dependence on the individual/family (their employer) for their visa, combined with the isolation of their work environment (particularly for those providing live-in care) from other workers and from organisational sources of support – including information and advice on employment rights – limited their ability to leave their employer. It likewise limited their rights of redress regarding irregular and exploitative working conditions.

These working conditions included long and undefined hours of work. With regard to weekly wages, given the long hours of care provided by live-in care workers, hourly rates of pay in some cases fell below the National Minimum Wage when accounting for the actual number of hours worked each week. Overtime work was sometimes unpaid and, in one case, wages were withheld by the employer. Irregular employment practices in private households also involved the avoidance of employer contributions to tax and national insurance payments. The irregular employment of migrant care workers in private households may have provided a means of cutting the costs of care for individuals and their families who were privately arranging their care. However, it potentially entailed considerable costs for their care workers, not least by preventing those who held temporary domestic worker visas from applying for permanent residency in the long term (as they would not have met the criteria of continual legal employment in the UK to be eligible to apply) and, therefore, from accessing rights of settlement.

Conclusion

The employment of migrant care workers in the UK and other European countries has been shaped by the restructuring of long-term care and policies towards immigration. As regards the former, ongoing cuts in public expenditure in the UK and elsewhere in Europe alongside growing demand for long-term care raise significant concerns for the public provision of long-term care services and for the provision of care labour. Labour costs make up a substantial proportion of the costs of providing long-term care. Care workers' wages account for half the costs of providing home care and between half and two-thirds of the costs in care homes, making the way in which long-term care is purchased and provided incredibly price-sensitive.[52] Pressures for cost containment – not simply to curtail public expenditure on care, but to increase the profits of major companies within long-term care markets – thus have implications for the wages and employment conditions of those who provide care, and for staff recruitment and retention difficulties in service provision. The shift towards the individual purchasing of care through a potentially growing reliance on the private funding of care also has implications for the direct employment of care workers by the individual or family in private households. By transferring responsibilities for the purchasing of care and the employment of care workers from the state to the individual, from the public to the private sphere, there is the potential for the growth of a far less regulated market of care work in private households. This has implications for both the quality of care and the quality of working conditions, in particular for workers whose rights are restricted through immigration controls.

Migrant labour may serve as a means to contain the costs of care in Western welfare states. However, political pressures to restrict immigration exist alongside pressures for cost containment. In the UK, labour migration policy has become increasingly restrictive under the points-based immigration system, targeting higher skilled workers while restricting the entry of skilled workers. With regard to care workers specifically, senior care workers are no longer categorised as a 'skilled' occupation in which the points-based immigration system recognises there to be labour shortages that should be addressed by temporary migrant workers. In addition, immigration policy regarding the entry, entitlement to work and length of stay of other categories of non-EEA nationals, including students and domestic workers, is becoming increasingly restrictive. At the same time, the temporary status of migrants in the UK is being reinforced more generally through restrictions on rights of settlement for non-EEA nationals, which may also compound unequal relations with employers in the context of care work.[53]

These developments point to conflicting interests at the level of state policies towards immigration and towards care – or potentially to the assumption that alternative sources of low-waged care workers can be drawn upon in place of migrant workers in the future. With regard to EEA workers, the number of EEA nationals entering care work in the UK (based on Worker Registration Scheme registrations) may currently be in decline.[54] As regards UK nationals, rising unemployment in the context of the economic recession may, in the short term, be expected to expand the potential pool of workers available to the care sector. However, the number of UK nationals entering care work may have to expand considerably to match the growth in the number of older people. In the long-term, restrictions on the recruitment of non-EEA workers may increase efforts to recruit other workers. However, if the care workforce is to nearly double in size to meet the needs of a growing older population, policy will need to rapidly address the factors that underpin recruitment and retention difficulties facing long-term care services. This raises much broader questions regarding the funding and quality of both long-term care provision and care work, and the viability of current models of care for older people to meet growing care needs in the future.

Acknowledgements

The research referred to in this chapter was carried out by Alessio Cangiano, Isabel Shutes and Sarah Spencer at the Centre on Migration, Policy and Society, University of Oxford. The work was supported by the a Lecturer in Social Policy. She has research interests in welfare states and migration; social divisions and inequalities; social care; and relations between the state, market and third sector.

Notes

1. Wittenberg, R., King, D., Malley, J., Pickard, L. and Comas-Herrera, A. 'Projections of Long-Term Care Expenditure in England under Different Assumptions Regarding the Future Balance between Residential and Home Care'. PSSRU Bulletin 19, Personal Social Services Research Unit, London School of Economics, London, 2010, p. 15.

2. Cangiano, A., Shutes, I., Spencer, S. and Leeson, G. *Migrant Care Workers in Ageing Societies: Research Findings in the UK*. Oxford: Centre on Migration, Policy and Society, University of Oxford, 2009; Österle, A. and Hammer, E. 'Care Allowances and the Formalization of Care Arrangements: The Austrian Experience'. In C. Ungerson and S. Yeandle (eds) *Cash for Care Systems in Developed Welfare States*. Basingstoke: Palgrave Macmillan, 2007; Walsh, K. and O'Shea, E. *The Role of Migrant Care Workers in Ageing Societies: Context and Experiences in Ireland*. Galway: Irish Centre for Social Gerontology, National University of Ireland, Galway, 2009; Bettio, F., Simonazzi, A. and Villa, P. 'Change in Care Regimes and Female Migration: The Care Drain in the Mediterranean'. *Journal of European Social Policy*, 16/3 (2006): 271–85; León, M. 'Migration and Care Work in Spain: The Domestic Sector Revisted'. *Social Policy and Society*, 9/3 (2010): 409–18.

3. Daly, M. and Lewis, J. 'The Concept of Social Care and the Analysis of Contemporary Welfare States'. *British Journal of Sociology*, 51/2 (2000): 281–98.

4. Bettio et al.: 'Change in Care Regimes and Female Migration: The Care Drain in the Mediterranean'; León: 'Migration and Care Work in Spain: The Domestic Sector Revisted'.

5. Williams, F. 'Towards a Transnational Analysis of the Political Economy of Care'. In R. Mahon and F. Robinson (eds) *Feminist Ethics and Social Policy: Towards a New Global Political Economy of Care*. Vancouver: University of British Columbia Press, 2011.

6. Williams, F. 'Converging Variations in Migrant Care Work in Europe'. *Journal of European Social Policy*, 22/4 (2012): 355–62; Williams, F. and Gavanas, A. 'The Intersection of Childcare Regimes and Migration Regimes: A Three-Country Study'. In H. Lutz (ed.) *Migration and Domestic Work*. Farnham: Ashgate, 2008.

7. Shutes, I. and Chiatti, C. 'Migrant Labour and the Marketisation of Care for Older People: the Employment of Migrant Care Workers by Families and Service Providers'. *Journal of European Social Policy*, 22/4 (2012): 392–405.

8. This chapter refers to England regarding the institutional context of long-term care for older people. A distinction is made where the data refer to England or to the UK.

9. Daly and Lewis: 'The Concept of Social Care and the Analysis of Contemporary Welfare States'. pp. 281–98; Pavolini, E. and Ranci, C. 'Restructuring the Welfare State: Reforms in Long-Term Care in Western European Countries'. *Journal of European Social Policy*, 18/3 (2008): 246–59.

10. Ungerson, C. 'Commodified Care Work in European Labour Markets'. *European Societies*, 5/4 (2003): 377–96.

11. Daly and Lewis: 'The Concept of Social Care and the Analysis of Contemporary Welfare States', pp. 281–98; Pavolini and Ranci: 'Restructuring the Welfare State: Reforms in Long-Term Care in Western European Countries', pp. 246–59.

12. Eborall, C., Fenton, W. and Woodrow, S. *The State of the Adult Social Care Workforce in England, 2010*. Leeds: Skills for Care, 2010.

13. Eborall et al.: *The State of the Adult Social Care Workforce in England, 2010.*

14. Eborall et al.: *The State of the Adult Social Care Workforce in England, 2010.*

15. Eborall et al.: *The State of the Adult Social Care Workforce in England, 2010.*

16. Eborall et al.: *The State of the Adult Social Care Workforce in England, 2010.*

17. Hussein, S. *Pay in Adult Social Care in England, Social Care Workforce Periodical 6.* London: Social Care Workforce Research Unit, King's College London, 2010.

18. Commission for Social Care Inspection. *The State of Social Care in England 2004–05.* London: Commission for Social Care Inspection, 2005.

19. Eborall, C. and Griffiths, D. *The State of the Adult Social Care Workforce in England, 2008.* Leeds: Skills for Care, 2008; Eborall et al.: *The State of the Adult Social Care Workforce in England, 2010.*

20. Eborall et al.: *The State of the Adult Social Care Workforce in England, 2010.*

21. Eborall et al.: *The State of the Adult Social Care Workforce in England, 2010.*

22. Forder, J. and Fernández, J.-L. *The Impact of a Tightening Fiscal Situation on Social Care for Older People.* Personal Social Services Research Unit Discussion Paper 2723, 2010.

23. Information Centre for Health and Social Care. *Personal Social Services Expenditure and Unit Costs, England 2009–10.* Leeds: Information Centre for Health and Social Care 2011.

24. Wanless, D. *Securing Good Care for Older People: Taking a Long-Term View.* London: King's Fund, 2006.

25. Commission on Funding of Care and Support. *Fairer Care Funding: The Report of the Commission on Funding of Care and Support,* 2011.

26. Commission for Social Care Inspection. *The State of Social Care in England 2006–07*. London: Commission for Social Care Inspection, 2008.

27. Forder and Fernández: *The Impact of a Tightening Fiscal Situation on Social Care for Older People*.

28. Ungerson, C. and Yeandle, S. (eds) *Cash for Care Systems in Developed Welfare States*. Basingstoke: Palgrave Macmillan, 2007.

29. Eborall et al.: *The State of the Adult Social Care Workforce in England, 2010*.

30. Eborall et al.: *The State of the Adult Social Care Workforce in England, 2010*.

31. Eborall et al.: *The State of the Adult Social Care Workforce in England, 2010*.

32. Forder 2007, cited in Eborall et al.: *The State of the Adult Social Care Workforce in England, 2010*, p. 28.

33. Eborall et al.: *The State of the Adult Social Care Workforce in England, 2010*.

34. Ruhs, M. and Anderson, B. (eds) *Who Needs Migrant Workers? Labour Shortages, Immigration and Public Policy*. Oxford: Oxford University Press, 2011.

35. Shutes, I. 'The Employment of Migrant Workers in Long-term Care: Dynamics of Choice and Control'. *Journal of Social Policy*, 41/1 (2012): 43–59.

36. Salt, J., *International Migration and the UK: Report of the UK SOPEMI Correspondent to the OECD, 2007*. London: Migration Research Institute, University College London, 2007, table 5.2.

37. Home Office, *Shortage Occupation List*. 2008, p. 5.

38. Cangiano et al.: *Migrant Care Workers in Ageing Societies: Research Findings in the UK*, p. 61.

39. Ruhs, M. and Anderson, B. 'Semi-compliance and Illegality in Migrant Labour Markets: An Analysis of Migrants, Employers and the State in the UK'. *Population, Space and Place*, 16/3 (2010): 195–221.

40. See Cangiano et al.: *Migrant Care Workers in Ageing Societies: Research Findings in the UK* for further details on the research.

41. Migrant workers were identified in the survey as foreign-born.

42. Categorised in the LFS as 'care assistants and home carers' which includes senior care workers and other workers in direct care providing jobs in residential care homes and home care services.

43. Cangiano et al.: *Migrant Care Workers in Ageing Societies: Research Findings in the UK*; Half of the foreign-born workforce in 2009 – care workers and nurses – have arrived since 2000.

44. Cangiano et al.: *Migrant Care Workers in Ageing Societies: Research Findings in the UK*.

45. Skills for Care. *National Minimum Data Set on Social Care Briefing 14: Migrant Workers*. Leeds: Skills for Care, 2011.

46. Skills for Care: *National Minimum Data Set on Social Care Briefing 14: Migrant Workers*.

47. Cangiano et al.: *Migrant Care Workers in Ageing Societies: Research Findings in the UK*.

48. Shutes: 'The Employment of Migrant Workers in Long-term Care: Dynamics of Choice and Control'. pp. 43–59.

49. Skills for Care: *National Minimum Data Set on Social Care Briefing 14: Migrant Workers*.

50. Interviewees were not able to identify whether their employers were in receipt of direct payments or were privately funding their care. However, given the limited number of older people in receipt of direct payments at the time of the research, employers were more likely to have been privately paying for their care.

51. This is not an indication of the immigration status of migrant care workers employed in private households in the UK overall, regarding which there is a lack of data.

52. Wanless: *Securing Good Care for Older People: Taking a Long-Term View*, p. xxv; Forder, J., Knapp, M., Hardy, B., Kendall, J., Matosevic, T. and Ware, P. 'Prices, Contracts and Motivations: Institutional Arrangements in Domiciliary Care'. *Policy and Politics*, 32 (2004): 207–22; Knapp, M., Hardy, B. and Forder, J.

'Commissioning for Quality: Ten Years of Social Care Markets in England'. *Journal of Social Policy*, 30/2 (2001): 283–306.

53. Anderson, B. 'Migration, Immigration Controls and the Fashioning of Precarious Workers'. *Work, Employment and Society*, 24/2 (2010): 300–17; Anderson, B. *Citizenship: What is it and Why Does it Matter?* Oxford: Migration Observatory, University of Oxford, 2011.

54. Cangiano et al.: *Migrant Care Workers in Ageing Societies: Research Findings in the UK.*

Further Reading

Ball, J. and Pike, G. *Black and Minority Ethnic and Internationally Recruited Nurses. Results from the RCN Employment/Working Well Surveys 2005 and 2002.* London: Royal College of Nursing, 2007.

Cangiano, A. and Shutes, I. 'Ageing, Demand for Care and the Role of Migrant Care Workers in the UK'. *Journal of Population Ageing*, 3/1–2 (2010): 39–57.

Spencer, S. *The Migration Debate.* Bristol: Policy Press, 2011.

CHAPTER 8

Irregular Immigration and the Underground Economy in Southern Europe: Breaking the Vicious Circle

Emilio Reyneri

Underground Economies and Unauthorised Immigrant Workers

With the exception of those seeking asylum for humanitarian reasons, undocumented[1] immigration arguably springs essentially from a strain between the restrictive labour immigration policies found in Southern European countries and a lively demand for foreign unskilled workers, grounded mainly (albeit not exclusively) in underground economies and their impact on labour markets as a whole.

In the late 1990s it became clear that the enforcement of immigration controls had managed to curb the clandestine entries across the region's sea borders at the southern and Adriatic coasts, but not the unauthorised influx of economic migrants, most of whom entered Western European countries by overstaying a tourist or alternative short-term visa – often moving to a country other than that which had granted them the visa, thanks to the Schengen free moving area.[2] A new hypothesis emerged to explain the extensive irregular immigration, centring on the existence of rooted underground economies that demand the labour of irregular migrants, unbound by the employment regulations of the country in question. The connection with the underground economy proves clear at a macro-level if we realise that, when including those who were later regularised, the number of undocumented immigrants is highest in the European countries where the domestic underground economy is most widespread and the demand for low-skilled labour is largest, as is the case in Southern

Europe. A good example of the contrary situation in Western Europe is Denmark, the country least entered by undocumented immigrants, because employment is strictly monitored and labour demand is biased towards highly skilled jobs.

At a micro-level, the hardships, expenses and sometimes great risk that entering the European countries through the 'back door' forces economic migrants to bear make the choice to try to enter those countries where they suppose it could be easy to make money even without a work permit an obvious one. Unauthorised immigrants are cut off from registered jobs and, were it not for the shelter of a large irregular labour market, they would soon be forced back to their home country. Fieldworkers support the hypothesis that before leaving their countries of origin many migrants had an understanding of how easy it would be to work without a proper permit in particular countries, thanks to information received either from the migratory chains of relatives and friends, or the network of smugglers who are generally needed to organise unauthorised migration.

European states are now deeply concerned about undocumented immigration, and the problems they face are only likely to get worse in the short term.[3] This is due to the expected impact of the ongoing economic crisis on the size of underground economies in European countries, with the dearth of official jobs pushing many individuals into undertaking and profiting from more informal transactions and work.[4] In the 'Fordist era' of the mid-twentieth century, the underground economy seemed destined to disappear, and the irregular status of many immigrants could look like a transitional phase without serious impact. This is not the case at present, given the ongoing 'casualisation' of employment, supplying both the motivation and the supply of workers required for the recovery of an underground economy.

Of the negative effects of this underground seam of immigrant labour, the financial burden is the most negligible, as unauthorised immigrants are entitled to claim only very few social services and, as consumers, pay value-added tax, meaning their costs could well be even lower than their contribution to the welfare state of the receiving countries.[5] Excluding the debatable question of criminality, it is the impact of casual immigrant work on the labour market that awakens the greatest worries. Some observers point out that in the short term undocumented immigration could even have positive effects, as it fills vacancies that would not be filled by native workers, even by those prone to work 'off-the-books', because of their poor working conditions, low compensation and scanty social prestige. However, as those labour shortages are in low productivity sectors and occupations, in the long run the effects would be negative, as employers can be less stimulated to introduce technological innovations. Moreover, the existence of a source of labour willing to carry out whichever poor job is available also risks throwing native unskilled workers into a 'race to the bottom', particularly within the countries whose labour demand is biased towards low-skilled jobs.

The Connection between Irregular Immigration and the South European Employment and Social Regimes

In all European countries, undocumented immigrants turn to the same sectors in which native irregular workers find employment: agriculture, construction, food processing, retail, hotels and catering, cleaning, transport and, finally, housekeeping and home elderly care. The latter is a particularly strong sector in countries with family-reliant welfare regimes where many personal services are not provided by public bodies, but paid for by families that do not self-produce them.[6] Employers in this sector are often small firms (which subcontract work) or individual households. The size of the underground economy is larger in countries where those low-skilled labour intensive sectors are more widespread, yet this is often shaped by the institutional arrangements and prevalent cultural attitudes within the country concerned. Comparative studies highlight the fact that underground economies are not linked to high levels of tax, but to the poor effectiveness of the public administration and to a lack of civic culture.[7] The best way to prevent employers from hiring workers 'off-the-books' is to inculcate a high level of 'tax morale'; that is, of compliance to pay taxes and social contributions rather than tightening controls, which must be supported by broad social consent to be effective.[8]

Underground economies are firmly rooted in South European countries in particular, as a result of their being largely tolerated by public opinion, and due to the close relationship either of compliance or of connivance of interest between employers and unregistered workers. While most unregistered workers find themselves in a position vulnerable to exploitation, some can earn close to the 'net wage' earned by regular workers, with less need for the welfare benefits provided as a result of paying taxes and social contributions. The former are forced to comply with their employers' decisions, as conflict risks their loss of work, without any alternative. For the most part, this unequal relationship prevails between undocumented immigrants and their employers, with a fear of contact with public authorities, which could result in their deportation and ban from re-entering the country, preventing any recourse to help in cases of exploitation.

To tackle the large pools of irregular immigrants, many South European countries have decided to implement mass regularisation drives. These had the consequence of making the connection between irregular workers and the underground economies that first gave them employment a transitory one. As recent research has highlighted in both Italy and Spain, few immigrant workers who availed themselves of regularisations went back to undocumented status, as most were able to renew their regularised temporary permit of stay for working reasons.[9] Thus, the underground economy seems to work well as a means of pulling unauthorised immigrants and of filtering them in order to provide the regular economy, through the amnesties, with immigrant workers who otherwise should not be able to enter the country.[10] This provides a route around the scarce legal entry channels and difficulties of offshore recruitment to find enough workers to meet the requirements of low-skilled job vacancies.

In almost all the European countries the immigration policy is more oriented towards filling highly skilled jobs (the so-called 'chosen immigration'), neglecting the many vacancies which exist also for regular low-skilled jobs, and which the native unemployed are either not able or not willing to fill. Thus, the quotas of entry targeted to fill low-skilled jobs are generally too scarce to meet real demand. Furthermore, within low-skilled job sectors the borders between regular and irregular labour markets are blurred, which fosters the entry and easy transfer of undocumented immigrants from one to the other. But even where the quotas for low-skilled jobs are fairly large, as was the case in Italy for some time, the serious difficulties of offshore recruitment pushed small firms and households, which are the main employers of low-skilled workers, to continue hiring immigrant workers 'off the street' or through personal relations. Offshore recruitment can be used to fulfil high-skilled vacancies with ease, as the selection can be based on educational and occupational curriculum; but for low-skilled roles in which the selection is generally based on personal characteristics and face-to-face relations, especially if the employers have 'to live' together with the employees either in a small firm or in a household, this is more difficult. Thus, small employers and households largely prefer to hire undocumented immigrant workers already living in the country; this also makes it easier to avoid any control and to recruit 'off-the-books'.

Framing Policies for Change

Given the clear demand for workers indicated by the significant employment, after amnesties, of previously irregular immigrants, new channels of regular entry must be provided. Furthermore, as unauthorised entries are promoted either by social networks or smugglers, policies must be adopted that could deter both social networks from supporting the further unauthorised entries of relatives and friends, and prospective economic immigrants from turning to expensive and risky organisations of smugglers.

Though four million immigrants have been regularised in the last 25 years, over two million undocumented immigrants are still living in the European Union, according to the EU-funded project

CLANDESTINO.[11] Most are irregular workers, whereas others are supported by relatives and friends. Though legislation usually allows for their deportation, legal and technical difficulties can hinder the implementation of forced return measures. Undocumented immigrants must be deported only to their country of origin, which must agree to readmit them. However, readmission agreements are stipulated with only certain countries of origin and often include several restrictions (for instance, a low limit to the number of people who can be deported on a weekly basis). The large numbers of undocumented immigrants present in the EU also make deportation a difficult option, given that it is discouraged by international law and that public opinion would rightly find it difficult to tolerate the large police raids and questioning that would be required within working spaces, including households, where most female irregular immigrants work. In several countries the undocumented population is too large and too incorporated within the economic and social systems to be removed coactively.[12]

Incentives for voluntary return similarly lack effectiveness, having in the past been targeted at regular immigrant workers who had lost jobs during the economic downturn. Few of those who were eligible availed themselves of them.

The sole policy tool which has effectively worked to drain a large pool of undocumented immigrant workers is the provision of amnesties that regularise extra-legal migrants. Regularisations are a sensitive issue, which divides experts and policymakers between pros and cons. As the International Migration Outlook asked in 2009: Is regularisation '[a] rewarding illegality or a necessary evil?'[13] Yet the more important question, arguably, is that of the trade-off between the advantages and the risks of the two types of amnesties.

Contrary to common belief in Southern Europe, many Central and North European countries have drawn on amnesties, albeit on a restricted and case-by-case basis. Some systems are based on discretionary decisions by administrative authorities, others either on the personal requirements of undocumented immigrants (based on factors such as the length of their continued stay in the country, family ties, social integration, nationality) or on a job offer by an employer.

In Germany, the asylum process was for a long time a functional equivalent of the South European mass amnesties.[14] Those 'pardon schemes' were under-emphasised by governments so as to evade public and political scrutiny, and also to prevent a 'pull effect' for new irregular entries looking for an easy regularisation. However, at the most they can prevent the build up of the number of unauthorised immigrants; they cannot clear out a huge pool of undocumented immigration on the scale that South European countries face.

South European countries have had to resort to recurrent large-scale regularisations (up to seven in Italy and Spain). All undocumented immigrants present in the country some weeks before the start of the procedure, who carried a clean criminal record and were able to show the proof of either a previous unregistered employment or a regular job offer by a perspective employer, were eligible to get a temporary (1–2 years) permit of stay and work. In Italy and Spain, the proportion of those who failed to avail themselves of the regularisation was estimated at around only 15 per cent, despite the employment restriction.

Yet how far have such regularisations been able to prevent migrants from lapsing into irregularity in the long term? In Italy and Spain the results of drives carried out in the 1980s and early 1990s were disappointing, as many regularised immigrants quickly relapsed into an undocumented status;[15] but the results of more recent regularisations have been different, as most regularised immigrant workers managed to retain their legal and occupational status even three years later (and this does not take into account those who went back home).[16] This suggests that the rising numbers of undocumented immigrants that were observed in Italy and Spain two to three years after regularisation were essentially caused by new unauthorised entries.

The second argument against the regularisations suggests that they can stimulate further irregular entries; and indeed, recurring regularisations may well have stimulated expectations of further amnesties, encouraging further unauthorised entries.[17] However, it is important to note that this negative effect is not necessarily implied in the existence of regularisations themselves, but is dependent on the accompanying migratory and labour policies.

The Economic Framework and Enforcement of Labour-Market Legislation

Amnesties are a necessary and pragmatic step to start a new approach to immigration and labour-market policies.[18] Yet stand-alone regularisations cannot, of course, break once and for all the connection between unauthorised immigration and underground economies. Policymakers seeking to tackle the problem in the long term must combine regularisation schemes not only with stronger border controls, as is usual, but above all with work to widen and improve authorised entries for economic immigrants and crack down on the underground economy. Therefore, the measures aimed at targeting irregular immigrant workers must be part of more general policies that deal with native firms and households employing native unregistered workers, and which seek to stem the tide of new unauthorised entries of immigrants looking for an unregistered job.

The range of measures detailed above could lead to the better implementation of existing rules on immigration. But they must, most vitally, be part of a broader policy against the unregistered employment both of foreign and native workers, which must be deeply legitimated by a widespread social and political consensus, a condition not easy in the Southern European countries where irregular economic behaviour is perceived as a 'victimless crime' and is largely tolerated. Thus, the involvement of social actors, especially trade unions and employers' associations, is fundamental.

Reducing taxes and social contributions that burden regular employment in low-productivity and low-skilled sectors of manufacturing and services, where unregistered jobs are most common, is one possible way to combat the underground economy. Governments should seek in the long term to replace domestic and family care services with a welfare regime in which most of those services are provided by either public or private organisations. In the short term, however, two lesser measures could be adopted also in familistic regimes to discourage informal hiring. A degree of tax relief should be allowed to households employing registered housekeepers and caregivers, and public subsidies for family care should be given to families as 'vouchers', which can be spent only on hiring registered workers, as in France.

New pathways of regular entry are required to channel prospective workers into filling low-skilled labour vacancies. A procedure used in many European countries provides that employers, directly or through employment offices, make an application to fill a vacancy with a specific worker still living abroad. The number of immigrants who can get a permit of entry in this way is subject to annual restrictions: either by sector or occupation or by country of origin. Yet this prevents small firms or households from judging candidates on less formal requirements based primarily on a face-to-face meeting. Furthermore, in being issued a work permit for a specific sector or occupation, migrant workers are prevented from moving between jobs, which risks their finding other irregular and taking on an extra-legal status. Therefore, after a fair period, immigrants should be allowed to replace their job-linked permit with a general permit of stay for working reasons.[19]

In order to prevent the vicious cycle of unauthorised immigration and irregular employment, a more innovative method of entry should be provided to deal at the same time with the high demand for low-skilled workers from small firms and households. One possible solution is the decoupling of the permit of stay from that of work, granting prospective immigrants a temporary permit allowing them a period of time (from 3 to 6 months) to look for a job. The number of job search permits should be fixed on a yearly basis and it could be broken down between the countries of emigration in case of bilateral agreements.[20] To satisfy the pressures of migratory chains, most of the applications should be allowed to those with relatives and friends living in the receiving country, who must engage themselves in supporting immigrants until they have found a job, and they should be liable to sanctions if they overstay when their visa expires.[21]

In order to coax underground economies into the light, regularisations for immigrants should be coupled with an amnesty for firms and households that employ 'off-the-books' native workers. Both the measures should be in principle employer-driven. However,

non-registered workers, both immigrants and natives, whose employers refuse to regularise their position, should be entitled to
denounce them and to start their own process of regularisation.
Domestic workers should also be allowed to start their own process,
as they are often employed by many households.

In the case of poorer regions or sectors, small financial rewards
could be provided to incentivise small firms and households to participate. Employers should pay a fine only if they refuse to hire a
worker whose prior employment relationship had been proven, in
which case the immigrant worker should get a temporary permit of
stay for job search. Of course, to involve as many unauthorised migrants as possible, those who apply for the regularisation should face
neither any penalty nor any risk of deportation. So generous should
be those large-scale extraordinary 'pardon schemes', and so rigorous
should be the following crackdown on firms and households who
would? employing workers without a contract.

The most critical change required in order to restrict the spread
of the underground economy is the enhancement and enforcement
of existing rules when they are breached by employers who refuse to
come forward, despite having had the opportunity to do so. Some
studies, mainly carried out in the USA, have suggested that sanctions
are of very limited effectiveness. However, the case of France in the
1990s shows that a strong enforcement of penalties and controls, combined with a wide campaign to mobilise public opinion, can produce
the desired results in some countries.[22] As a matter of fact, the success of the sanctions against employers depended on how they are
implemented.[23]

When it comes to strong enforcement, a lack of focus and resolve
is manifested. Sanctions against employers must be intelligently po-
liced and constantly fine-tuned to keep up with real changes in the
behaviour of evaders. Yet in nearly all the European countries, and
especially in the southern ones, inadequate resources are devoted to
enforcing rules against irregular employment, due to a gap between
the number of labour inspectors in proportion to the number of firms
and the ILO's benchmark for this ratio.[24] The EU directive encour-
ages member states to determine a yearly target for the number of

inspections; however, the proposal for a target of 10 per cent of all firms was not included in the final draft; thus, the extent to which enforcement targets will make the jump from theory into practice is tentative.[25] Furthermore, there is a serious problem for private households, which are rarely checked, although many unregistered employees work in domestic services. The protection of private living space is generally guaranteed by constitutions, but a solution should be found shifting the responsibilities of the inspections in households to customs officers, as has previously been suggested in Germany.

In line with this, enforcement must avoid the present danger of forcing unauthorised immigrants, when caught, to shoulder the greater part of both the blame and the consequences. If unauthorised immigrants caught working 'off-the-books' are sentenced to be deported, as in most European countries, not only will they avoid lodging complaints against their employers but they will cooperate with them to escape controls. Moreover, in case the irregular employment is caught by inspections, unauthorised immigrant workers risk both not being able to testify against employers and missing their deserved remuneration payment. To avoid this risk the EU directive provides that the deportation must be suspended during the course of legal proceedings and that a permit of stay linked to the length of proceedings can be granted in case of criminal offences. Those provisions go some way to increasing the protection of unauthorised immigrants, but they are too limited if we want to facilitate cooperation between these migrants and public authorities in filing complaints against firms and households employing them 'off-the-books'. To enable this, 'rewarding legislation' is required, as it occurs for the victims of human trafficking. Unauthorised immigrant workers who file a complaint against their illegal employers should, to this end, be granted a temporary permit to search for work and could be entitled to receive support services to help with both this and the legal proceedings.

In addition, penalties should be tough enough to pose a serious disincentive for employers. In many European countries there is a tendency towards more severe sanctions, resulting from the 2009 directive of the European Parliament on 'measures against employers of illegally staying third-country nationals'. In the case of repeated and serious infringements, EU member states are required to impose not only fines and other financial sanctions (exclusion from public tenders and subsidies, temporary or permanent closure of economic activity), but also 'effective, proportionate and dissuasive criminal penalties'; some countries go so far as to impose imprisonment as a penalty (up to three years in France and five years in Spain).[26] Of course, employers who subcontract to other firms should be considered fully liable for their infringements and should be financially sanctioned, just as their subcontractors are.

Enforcing all the above-mentioned measures might prevent the recovery of the vicious circle of unauthorised immigration and irregular employment after an amnesty dried up the previous pool of unauthorised immigrants. Of course, a strong political will is required. Cracking down on underground economy is easier said than done.

Notes

1. Undocumented, unauthorised and irregular are used synonymously to denote economic immigrants living in a European country without a work permit.

2. Many visa-overstayers in Italy, Spain, Portugal and Ireland were granted a tourist visa in Germany. See REGINE. *Regularisations in Europe, Final Report.* JLS/B4/2007/05. Vienna: International Centre for Migration Policy Development, 2009.

3. Junkert, C. and Kreienbrink, A. 'Irregular Employment of Migrant Workers in Germany'. In M. Kupiszewski and H. Mattila (eds) *Addressing the Irregular Employment of Immigrants in the European Union: Between Sanctions and Rights.* Geneva: IOM, 2008; Sciortino, G. 'The Regulation of Undocumented Migration'. In M. Martiniello and J. Rath (eds) *International Migration and Immigrant Incorporation: The Dynamics of Globalization and*

Ethnic Diversity in European Life. Amsterdam: Amsterdam University Press, 2010.

4. http://www.econ.jku.at/members/Schneider/files/publications/ LatestResearch2010/ShadEcOECD2010.pdf.

5. Of course that problem is serious for asylum seekers and refugees who, however, have nothing to do with undocumented immigrants for economic reasons. See Boeri, T., McCormick, B. and Hanson, G. (eds) *Immigration Policy and the Welfare System.* Oxford: Oxford University Press, 2002; Schönwälder, K., Vogel, D. and Sciortino, G. *Migration and Illegality in Germany.* Berlin: WZB, 2006.

6. Esping-Andersen, G. *Social Foundations of Postindustrial Economies.* Oxford: Oxford University Press, 1999.

7. OECD. *Employment Outlook.* Paris: OECD, 2004.

8. Alm, J. and Torgler, B. 'Culture Differences and Tax Morale in the United States and in Europe'. *Journal of Economic Psychology*, 27/2 (2006): 224–46.

9. REGINE: *Regularisations in Europe*, Final Report.

10. OECD. *International Migration Outlook.* Paris: OECD, 2009.

11. Vogel, D. *Size and Development of Irregular Migration to the EU.* Comparative Policy brief CLANDESTINO project, 2009. http:// clandestino.eliamep.gr/wp-content/uploads/2009/12/clandestino _policy_brief_comparative_size-of-irregular-migration.pdf.

12. Sciortino: *International Migration and Immigrant Incorporation: The Dynamics of Globalization and Ethnic Diversity in European Life.*

13. OECD: *International Migration Outlook.*

14. Finotelli, C. 'Accolti o sanati? L'asilo e la protezione umanitaria in paesi di "nuova" e "vecchia" immigrazione'. In F. Decimo and G. Sciortino (eds) *Reti migranti.* Bologna: Il Mulino, 2006.

15. Reyneri, E. *Migrants' Involvement in Irregular Employment in the Mediterranean Countries of the European Union.* International Migration Papers no. 39, Geneva: ILO, 2001.

16. REGINE: *Regularisations in Europe*, Final Report.

17. Sciortino: *International Migration and Immigrant Incorporation: The Dynamics of Globalization and Ethnic Diversity in European Life.*

18. Levinson, A. 'Why Countries Continue to Consider Regularization'. In *Migration Information Source.* Migration Policy Institute, September 2005; Sumption, M. *Policies to Curb Unauthorized Employment.* European University Institute and Migration Policy Institute, May 2011.

19. Kupiszewki, M. 'Addressing the Irregular Employment of Migrants. Concluding Remarks and Recommendations'. In M. Kupiszewki and H. Mattila (eds) *Addressing the Irregular Employment of Immigrants in the European Union: Between Sanctionsand Rights.* Geneva: IOM, 2008.

20. Kupiszewki: 'Addressing the Irregular Employment of Migrants. Concluding Remarks and Recommendations'.

21. That procedure was adopted in Italy for two years, but no information is available concerning its outcome.

22. Marie, C. V. *Measures Taken to Combat the Employment of Undocumented Foreign Workers in France.* In OECD. *Combating the Illegal Employment of Foreign Workers.* Paris: OECD, 2000.

23. Martin, P. and Miller, M. J. *Employer Sanctions: French, German and US Experiences,* International Migration Papers no. 36, Geneva: ILO, 2000.

24. Andrees, B., Hancilova, B. and Wickramasekara, P. 'Irregular Employment of Migrants: An ILO Perspective'. In M. Kupiszewki and H. Mattila (eds), *Addressing the Irregular Employment of Immigrants in the European Union: Between Sanctions and Rights.* Geneva: IOM, 2008.

25. Sciortino: *International Migration and Immigrant Incorporation: The Dynamics of Globalization and Ethnic Diversity in European Life.*

26. But Ireland, Denmark and the United Kingdom have exercised their right to opt-out and are not subject to the Directive.

Further Reading

Entorf, H. 'Rational Migration Policy Should Tolerate Non-Zero Illegal Migration Flows: Lessons from Modelling the Market for Illegal Migration'. *International Migration*, Migration, 40/1 (2002): 27–43.

Kupiszewki, M. and Mattila, H. (eds) *Addressing the Irregular Employment of Immigrants in the European Union: Between Sanctions and Rights*. Geneva: IOM, 2008.

CHAPTER 9

Restricting the Right to Family Migration in Denmark: When Human Rights Collide with a Welfare State under Pressure

Emily Cochran Bech and Per Mouritsen[1]

Introduction

By their very definition, liberal welfare states must seek to protect both the individual right to a family life and the state's capacity to maintain and promote its citizens' welfare. Yet these goals are increasingly perceived to be in tension with one another. Family migration contributes to a weakening of the welfare contributor-to-recipient ratio, so the argument goes, by broadening the pool of likely welfare recipients without correspondingly growing the number of active contributors to welfare. The common conclusion is that family migration must be restricted to protect the welfare system and the overall economic potential of the society within an increasingly competitive global market, with individual rights to a family life becoming a regrettable but necessary casualty. In opposition to this are those who maintain that some such rights should take precedence over concerns about their economic consequences, and furthermore that curbing those rights is not helpful, economically or otherwise, to the longer-term future of a society.

Economic hard times naturally put extra pressure on the welfare state, incentivising government to do whatever possible to shield the welfare system from stresses possibly caused by family migration. However, this chapter traces restrictive developments in Danish family migration policy that actually pre-date the economic crisis of the late 2000s. The welfare protection arguments have been used through periods of state budget surplus and deficit, ushering in the most restrictive family migration policies in Europe and possibly in the world. These policies have been targeted by human rights scholars for denying basic family rights on the basis of age, national origin, education and socio-economic status, even as restrictions on immigration were further heightened by policymakers. The debates around these developments have focused not only on economic but on value-based goals such as hindering forced (and arranged) marriages among young people from migrant backgrounds, centring on how best to selectively cultivate the ideal of migrants as integrated and willing 'contributor-citizens', who will strengthen the existing Danish welfare society.

This chapter analyses the family-migration-related discourse and policy of the 2001–11 Liberal-Conservative government in Denmark, which may in retrospect be seen as an experiment in subjugating family reunification rights to the greater goal of sustaining the welfare state, rather than as an attempt to balance the two. This reordering of priorities – with even family reunification policies becoming explicitly linked to labour-market demand for high-skilled workers, and to the goal of reducing strains on the welfare system – may turn out to have been short-lived in its most extreme form, at least.

However, though at this writing the subsequent centre-left government is repealing some of the most restrictive policies instituted prior to 2011, the paradigm of the competition welfare state still stands in Denmark and multiple other countries, and it is likely to continue to spark conflicts between states' attempts to control family migration, their own liberal commitments and the international rights conventions to which they have agreed.

Danish Family Reunification Policy – Restriction and Screening

Prior to 2000, Danish family reunification policy was primarily based on the individual's right to family life, and thus for new and existing spouses to migrate along with children and, to a more limited extent, other family members. In 2000, this normal right to spousal reunification was withdrawn for individuals between 18 and 25 years of age when parliament passed a law specifying that, for this age group, a residence permit would only be granted for spousal reunification if the marriage in question was evaluated to be undoubtedly entered into according to both partners' wishes.[2] In 2002, an overhaul of Danish immigration and integration law solidified this withdrawal with an absolute requirement that all applicants (i.e. both partners) must be over 24 years old to be granted spousal reunification. These policy changes were quite clearly intended to deter family establishment by young adults who would have married young spouses from their families' home regions and brought them to Denmark. The politicians behind the laws defended them on the particular grounds that they would prevent forced marriages with partners to be brought from other countries.

In addition to the so-called '24-year rule', the minority Liberal-Conservative government and the supporting Danish People's Party's 'Firm and Fair Immigration Policy' introduced significant additional conditions for spousal reunification concerning:

- **The couple's connection to Denmark**
  - All couples where the Danish resident or citizen partner had not been a Danish citizen for 28 years would be *required to have a stronger connection (as a couple) to Denmark than to any other country.*
  - Lawmakers kept a requirement that foreign citizens without refugee status should have had permanent residency for three years before applying for reunification entry of a spouse, but raised the minimum time in Denmark required to take on permanent residency to a minimum of seven years of legal residence.[3] This meant that *many foreign citizens would need to have lived in Denmark for ten years prior to applying for family reunification of a spouse,* as opposed to the previous six.
- **A real (and non-abusive) marriage/partnership**
  - Both partners must have been *physically present at the marriage* and have entered into it *voluntarily,* and the spouses or partners *must live together.*
  - While the previous law had required immigration authorities to consider the entire case in terms of whether the marriage was

to be deemed *pro forma*, the 2002 law allowed applications for spousal reunifications to be *rejected where it could be determined that the 'primary' objective of a marriage at its start was to allow one partner to get residence in Denmark* – whether or not other aspects of the marriage indicated that it was otherwise a real partnership.[4]

o   The Danish-resident partner *must not have been sentenced to jail time for domestic violence* within the previous 10 years.

- **Evidence of capacity for welfare independence**
    o   The couple must provide evidence for a *bank guarantee or deposit of 50,000 DKK as a caution against any support payments* to the new entrant from the public welfare system.
    o   The *requirement that the Danish-resident spouse be able to financially support the incoming spouse was expanded from foreign-citizen residents to all applicants,* including Nordic and Danish citizens.[5]
    o   The Danish-resident applicant *must not have received social support payments during the previous year.*
    o   The Danish-resident applicant must be in *possession of his/her own (rented or owned) place of residence (with a few exceptions allowed)* with at least 20 m^2 (215 $ft.^2$) per inhabitant.

The aim of the 2002 immigration policies was, according to the parties involved in pushing for the legislation, to reduce the numbers of family reunification migrants and refugees granted asylum, whilst raising the number of student and work-related immigrants, in part to allow the government to focus on the integration of migrants already in the country.[6] There were thus two primary family migration goals of the policies. First, to deter family *establishment* by young adults marrying partners from other countries, targeting arranged and forced marriages from major immigrant source countries in particular. This goal was the more emphasised in political debate. And second, to prevent the *reunification* of less economically well-established Danish citizens and residents to their spouses. As the government itself has declared, the policies have certainly effected a change in numbers of applications for and residence permits granted on the basis of family reunification.

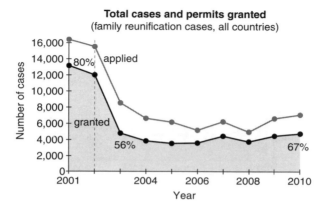

FIGURE 9.1   Family reunification in Denmark: applications submitted and permits granted.
Source: Danish Integration Ministry.

The Impact of the 2002 Policies

The 2002 policy changes led to a substantial reduction in family immigration. Between 2001 and 2003, the number of reunification permits granted to spouses fell from about 6,500 (about two thirds of all applicants) to about 2,500 (less than half of all applicants). Residence permits granted each year for family reunification fell from 12,571 in 2001, with an acceptance rate of 80 per cent, to 4,768 in 2010, with an acceptance rate of 67 per cent.

As was intended, the policies affected applicants from certain countries more drastically than those from others, by deterring people from applying in the first place and by lowering the rate at which applicants were granted entrance. Applicants from Somalia and Turkey experienced the greatest decrease in residence permits proportionate to applications made, while the rate of acceptance for Iraqis was only somewhat reduced between 2001 and 2010. Thai applicants continued to experience quite a high rate of acceptance after the change.

Additionally, the average marriage age of first- and second-generation immigrants from non-Western countries has risen somewhat, with fewer marrying between the ages of 17 and 21 in 2009 than married within the same age bracket in 2001, prior to the policy

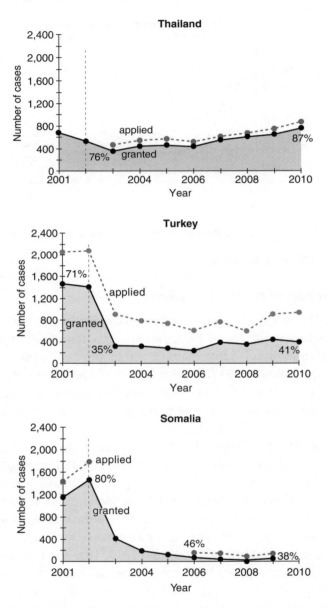

FIGURE 9.2   Family reunification applications to Denmark from four nationalities, and permits granted.
Source: Statistics Denmark, Danish Integration Ministry.

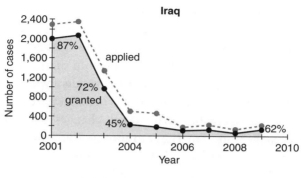

FIGURE 9.2   (*Continued*)

changes. The Danish Integration Ministry considers this change to be 'a result of the change in family reunification rules'.[7] A report by researchers at the Danish National Centre for Social Research qualifies this somewhat by pointing to the general upward trend in marriage age and the education levels of young immigrants and women descended from migrants, which began before 2002, meaning the impact of the tougher immigration policies of the last decade has possibly been weaker than is sometimes claimed.[8] However, the report itself was forced to acknowledge the effect of the new rules, in causing the marriage age amongst migrant communities to rise significantly since 2002. Before the changes, a little over 30 per cent of 21-year old minority women were married, the report points out, in comparison to the 10 per cent of the same age bracket that are married after the changes.

The policies have also had an effect on *who* immigrants, their descendants and – to a lesser extent – ethnic Danes marry. They seem to have significantly reduced the proportion of first- and second-generation immigrants from non-Western countries, who wed individuals resident in another country at the time of the marriage, from 61.1 per cent of those married in 2001 to 24.9 per cent in 2009.[9] Yet, according to a large qualitative interview study by Garbi Schmidt, Professor of Culture and Identity at Roskilde University, and her fellow researchers, this does not mean more ethnic-minority individuals are marrying people of other ethnic-minority or ethnic-Danish backgrounds. Before and after the rule changes, only 3 per cent of ethnic minority young adults aged 20–23 married outside their own ethnic groups, and only slightly more of those aged 24–27 did so.[10] The study also reported only a small growth in marriages to others within the same minority ethnic group, but resident within Denmark (as opposed to same-group individuals living elsewhere), though the rise is so small that its attribution to the rule changes is in doubt. Interestingly, this higher rate of marriage to another young person from the same minority group and already living in Denmark was particularly notable among young people of Turkish origin, which the report's authors attribute to the greater availability of Turkish marriage partners in Denmark and because, ironically, marriage at a young age is prioritised especially highly for young Turkish women. The report, therefore, concludes that the rule changes' biggest effect is that many minority young people who might have married an overseas spouse and applied for their entry before the changes seem to be choosing not to marry at all.

In addition to influencing whether, when and whom young minorities and even ethnic Danes marry, the rule changes seem to have had an effect on where and how those who do marry foreigners live out their family life. Many in Denmark with foreign spouses chose to move to Sweden, due in large part to that country's more liberal immigration policies. A 2005 study by the Øresund Bridge Consortium and the Öresund Committee (who manage the countries' connecting bridge and the possibilities for easy movement between the Copenhagen and Malmö regions) found that of about 3,300 people who had moved from Denmark to the Skåne region of Sweden in 2004 alone, nearly 20 per cent cited the Danish family reunification rules as an important factor in their move.[11]

The economic effects of the rule changes remain somewhat uncertain, since they are shaped by the country's labour market and welfare system, in addition to the immigration policies themselves. On the one hand, substantially fewer family reunifications have been granted under the new rules, especially from countries whose previous family migrants tended to be less educated. This suggests that the changes have likely had a positive economic effect on the Danish system as a whole by producing less strain on the welfare and educational systems. On the other hand, the rules have caused many people to move to Sweden, thus taking their returns on the Danish welfare system's investments in them elsewhere (though some who have moved may continue to commute to jobs in Denmark). Finally, the rules seem to combine with other immigration and integration rules to contribute more generally to a negative feeling, within and outside Denmark, of the country being closed and somewhat inhospitable toward foreigners. In some cases this may be said to dissuade numerous Danish-foreign couples from settling in the country, and foreign workers, more broadly, from wanting to stay in the long-term.[12]

After the major changes to family reunification policy in 2002, the rules received only minimal adjustment until the autumn of 2010 and spring of 2011, when the Liberal-Conservative government and the Danish People's Party introduced two phases of further restrictions that are expected to drastically influence the number of family reunifications which are granted. The government declared that while the existing rules had 'had a very significant and positive effect', the absence of any requirements concerning the qualifications of the incoming family member had meant that there were too many admitted spouses who 'have difficulty integrating and with that adapting to Danish values, and who have difficulty in entering the Danish labour market'.[13] The time had come, they argued, to

> make new concrete demands that the individual spouse-reunited foreigner, as a condition for spousal reunification, be in possession of integration-relevant qualifications that also make the reunited spouse capable of contributing to the Danish society, thus supporting integration and the agreeing parties' agreement for growth and prosperity.[14]

To do so, the government and its support party changed rules to further restrict the number and profile of family reunifications by:

- Reducing overall numbers of applications submitted by increasing the application fee (from 5,975 DKK in 2010 to 7,775 DKK, or about $1,400) and raising the bank guarantee required for the couple to furnish in order to serve as security against any welfare payments (from 63,413 to 100,000 DKK, or about $18,000).

- Raising the bar for the couple's ties to Denmark the couple would be required to have 'substantially greater ties to Denmark' than to the other country in question.
- Replacing the previous hard-and-fast 24-year rule with a new exam and points system requiring the foreign-resident spouse to have 'integration-eligible' qualifications. The applicant would be required to:
  - Take and pass an Immigration Test assessing basic Danish language and cultural proficiency within three months of gaining residency, paying an examination fee of 3,000 DKK (about $550).[15]
  - Qualify for family reunification through a points system taking language competency, education level and institution, career field, and work experience into account; spouses under 24 may now qualify, but only with twice as many points as are required of those 24 or older.
- The Danish-resident spouse, if not a citizen, would be required to fulfil all the current (from 2010) requirements for gaining permanent residency, even if he/she gained permanent residency under more lenient rules. For example, the Danish-resident spouse must, among other things, speak and write Danish with high proficiency (B1–B2 level, according to the European standard), not have received welfare more than six months in the previous three years, show significant civic engagement or have passed a civic knowledge exam, and have either worked three and one half of the previous four years *or* have completed an education in Denmark *or* have passed an even higher (B2 level) Danish exam.

The policies were implemented in two phases, with an entry exam and initial fee raise put into effect on 1 January 2011 and a later stiffening of the exam requirements, further raising of the fee and required guarantee, more stringent measures of ties to Denmark and the points system finally put in force on 1 July 2011. These changes significantly reduced the number of applications throughout 2011 as well as the proportion of accepted applications from those who do apply. While in the first quarter of 2009 and 2010 there were 1,538 and 1,670 applications submitted, respectively, after the initial phase implemented in January 2011 only 927 applications were submitted in the first quarter of that year by Danish residents to bring family members into the country – a decrease of 40–45 per cent.[16] Lars Kyhnau Hansen, leader of Marriage Without Borders, a Danish interest organisation for international couples' rights, expected on the passage of the law change that the phase-in of the even more restrictive rules would likely cause 'something like a near-total stop' to family reunifications to Denmark.[17]

This course of progressive restriction halted, however, with the September 2011 election of a new centre-left government. It has kept some of the previous government's changes (such as the 24-year rule and self-support requirements) but repealed the prohibitive fees and the most restrictive residence and testing requirements. It has also lifted some of the strictest requirements for the Danish-resident spouses to achieve permanent residency (and thereby the right to a spouse's entry), lowering requirements for which language exam must be passed and for proven civic involvement, as well as including more exceptions for extenuating circumstances (for example for refugees with injuries from past trauma). It remains to be seen what effect this scaling back of the sharpest restrictions will have on family immigration to the country going forward.

The Right to Family Life and Protection from Discrimination: Human Rights and Family Reunification

In November 1950 Denmark was one of twelve initial signatories to the European Convention on Human Rights (ECHR), whose Article 8 states that

1. *Everyone has the **right to respect for his private and family life**, his home and his correspondence.*

2. *There **shall be no interference by a public authority with the exercise of this right except such as** is in accordance with the law and is necessary in a democratic society **in the interests of national security, public safety or the economic well-being of the country,***

for the prevention of disorder or crime, for the protection of health or morals, or for the protection of the rights and freedoms of others.[18]

The convention thus protects the right to family, but states that the right is not absolute. Yet in practice the interference by public authorities in the exercise of the right must not only be legal and necessary for the purposes stated, but its invasiveness must also be *proportional* to the purpose for which it is undertaken; thus, the European Court of Human Rights normally weighs individual interests versus state interests.[19]

The ECHR also forbids discrimination on the basis of (a non-exhaustive list of) certain grounds, though this is not normally interpreted by the European Court of Human Rights to include different treatment of a state's citizens and non-citizen residents, nor of EU and non-EU citizens.[20]

Protection from discrimination, as detailed in several United Nations conventions to which Denmark is a signatory, is also relevant here: discrimination on the basis of race, skin colour, national or ethnic origin, handicap and gender is forbidden.[21]

The Danish family reunification policies introduced over the last decade have been criticised for their potential violations of these two protected aspects of human rights: respect for family life and freedom from discrimination. Human rights experts have focused on several aspects of the policies that threaten these rights.

And in respect to all these changes there is another overall concern about the frequent changing of the law in this area. Individuals are not given reasonable possibilities, say critics, to be able to anticipate their rights and responsibilities under the system of family migration rules. Most recently, the (mid-2011) changes implementing a new and stricter version of the language and knowledge exam for entry, as the Danish Institute for Human Rights points out in a response to the law proposal, are likely to leave applicants uncertain of what to expect and whether they can expect to be able to attain residency. In addition, the quick change to the exam only a few months after its introduction, and with very little data available as to how the first version has worked, leaves open the question as to whether the increased restriction is necessary for its purpose.[22]

Keeping the basic right to family life in view, human rights experts (and some of the parties who have now won government power) have also objected to some of the family migration rules due to their potential for discriminating on the basis of socio-economic status and disability, by making the right to family immigration contingent on individuals' ability to prove employment and housing status, pay disproportionately high application fees and meet somewhat difficult education and language requirements. This potential for discrimination, say critics, lies in both the fees, financial requirements, language tests and educational point systems for both permanent residency (which the Danish-resident family member must fulfil if not a citizen) and for spousal immigration.[23] Some individuals, due to lesser abilities, handicaps or difficult financial circumstances, may never be able to fulfil the requirements to achieve spousal reunification. A related problem is that while refugees are excepted from some family immigration requirements, the law is unclear on whether Danish-resident spouses who came as refugees also need to fulfil the permanent residency requirements.[24] This is especially of concern since refugees are commonly diagnosed as suffering from post-traumatic stress disorder and may consequently be unable to meet them.

And finally, the Danish Institute for Human Rights raises the concern that requiring all non-citizen resident spouses applying for spousal reunification to meet the very strict, points-based permanent residency requirements (even if they attained permanent residency under previous rules) may constitute illegal discrimination against non-citizens if there are no substantive grounds for applying those rules to non-citizens but not to citizens. The points system's requirements on the basis of education, employment, self-support and lack of criminal record, it is argued, may be relevant to citizens as well as non-citizens.[25]

Interestingly, in a twist within immigration policy debates, the Danish state's restrictive access to citizenship may combine with developing European rights standards for non-citizens resident in EU states to tie the Danish and other governments' hands somewhat in terms of family reunification policy. Since the European human rights standards and common policy on migration (in which Denmark does not currently participate) increasingly protect the rights of refugees, EU- and candidate-country nationals and even some third-country nationals living in EU state territory, restrictive national family migration regimes may not be able to control family reunification policy as tightly for non-nationals as for their own citizens. Since Denmark may join its fellow EU member states in participating in these policy standards more fully (which has been mentioned more and more in the run-up to a coming period of Danish chairmanship of the EU), restrictive policies in both citizenship and family reunification policies have the potential to put citizens at a disadvantage.

Sustaining Welfare: The Contribution Ideal

Political arguments about the recent restrictions of the right to family reunification reflect in large part a broader discourse on immigration and integration, which, however, has gone through a series of stages. The 2002 restrictions, particularly the 24-year rule, were legitimised not only as an attempt to protect young people of Middle Eastern origin from arranged or forced marriages to homeland spouses who were alien to Danish egalitarian values, but also relatively openly as an effective way to curb migration in order to more effectively integrate those already in the country. While these concerns remain salient, there has been a shift toward emphasis on ideals of individual contribution to the welfare state as well as overall financial sustainability and growth.

Concern for the welfare state (or 'welfare society') was always central to Danish immigration discourse. Historically the project of the Social Democrats, but since World War II representing a consensus across left, right and centre, the welfare state has been regarded as the motor of substantial civic equality. Social levelling and material safety, free education, gender equality and state-subsidised child care make up one side of a contract. The other is a set of civic expectations, key among them that all, including women, stand ready to work and pay tax, and increasingly also to participate and volunteer in civil society and local institutions.

As elsewhere in Scandinavia, equality and welfare-state participation are part of the very fabric of nationhood, legitimising a continuing project of integration that began with the working class and women and now aims to include immigrants.[26] Because they are so strongly institutionally embedded, the ideals of this project, while emphasising work, education and social equality, also require and produce significant cultural homogeneity – and tend to reinforce acculturation and conformity of newcomers as a 'functional' policy ideal. Being a welfare citizen becomes a way of life that must be taught.

The ideal of reciprocity, where everybody benefits and contributes, is, however, increasingly challenged by the growing number of citizens who, through physical or mental illness, lack of skills, or early retirement, participate in only one side of the work-and-welfare contract. This challenge may also be witnessed in the subtly changing emphases over the last three decades in the discourse and policy of 'welfare-state integration' of immigrants, and their interaction with value-oriented and culturalist elements.[27] Although the welfare-state burden was a far-right-wing trope already in the 1970s and 1980s, until the late eighties official and mainstream political discourse was dominated by concerns with equal opportunity and rights, such as how immigrants as a vulnerable group with certain handicaps (including cultural distance) could be helped into society.[28] This changed from the early 1990s, when government reports and parliamentary debates placed increasing emphasis on immigrants becoming self-supporting and productive. The development culminated in the 1999 Social Democratic *Integration Law*, which, placing the obligation to integrate squarely on immigrants rather than the receiving society, would 'contribute to the newly arrived foreigner's possibility for participating on an equal footing with other citizens in the political, economic, work-related, social, religious and cultural life of society'.[29]

This discourse was less about economic sustainability and more about a social democratic ideal of civic recognition and dignity and preserving a special Danish model of solidarity for which Danish workers had toiled in the past. Its moralising emphasis on duties before rights was further intensified with the 2001–11 Liberal-Conservative government, which combined tough neo-liberal *quid-pro-quo* economic and legal incentives and punishments for (un)successful labour-market integration,[30] with a more 'republican' discourse on demonstrated commitment and willingness to make an effort and become part of Danish society. Under this government, pushed forward by the Danish People's Party, the integration requirements spilled over into citizenship and residence policy. Now employment and self-sufficiency, language proficiency, historical/cultural knowledge courses and tests, loyalty affirmation and Danish value declarations, and eventually 'active participation', for example in voluntary associations and sports clubs, were added to the conditions of membership.[31] This development – which occurred in overlapping stages from neo-Durkheimian work and basic liberal values, to tougher neo-liberal sticks-and-carrots, to the testing of liberal-democratic credentials, to 'good' citizenship and even ethno-national acculturation – has put Denmark in a position as a distinct immigration and integration hardliner in Europe.

However, the recent development in family reunification policy, the focus of this chapter, appears to be connected to a new turn visible in this development. The last few years and the recent 2011 election have seen diminishing right-wing returns on populist political investments in playing the foreigner card, with electoral majorities seemingly convinced that 'enough is enough' (but also that restrictive policies by and large should remain in place). On the one hand, Lars Løkke Rasmussen, the liberal prime minister who succeeded Anders Fogh Rasmussen in 2009, was less inclined to promote the more national-culturalist elements of the integration agenda, and the new social democratic-led government – which will not depend on the Danish People's Party – is also likely to adopt a more pragmatic stance. On the other hand, since the international financial crisis in 2008 the immigration discourse has become intensely focused on labour-market integration and education. Now, however, the moralistic onus on reciprocity and worthiness is giving way to hard-and-fast concern with the sustainability of the welfare state and questions about the economic 'net benefit' of welfare supports.

This concern has also been echoed in recurring political appeals – starting as early as 2002 – and several serious attempts by economists of various stripes to calculate whether and to what extent immigrants have or have not been a net economic burden.[32] These attempts provoked foreseeable controversy, for instance over the reasonable-ness of including political refugees, over immigrant populations being younger and hence presently more costly in education and childcare, and concerning whether similar calculations were in order in the case of other groups whose net contribution to the Danish state might itself be doubted, such as the Danish People's Party's own voters.

A survey of political debate over the presentation in November 2010 by the previous centre-right government and Danish People's Party of a new family reunification policy, *New Times, New Demands*, and subsequent legislation in early 2011 indicates the high saliency of arguments about economic growth and using 'objective criteria' of 'integration potential'. As the minister presenting the legislation emphasised its motivation, 'Denmark wants to attract foreigners who can demonstrate civic values and create growth and prosperity'. Indeed, the law proposal stated, 'The government and Danish People's Party have agreed that Danish immigration policy will from now on have the clear and new target that Denmark as a rule will only make room for those foreigners who can and wish to contribute to growth and prosperity in Denmark'.[33] The government's ministers and supporting legislators repeatedly emphasised the need to apply the contribution-for-growth criteria to family migrants as well as oth-ers. 'I can confirm that we are working on a point system', said Conser-vative politician Naser Khader in 2010 about the development of new family reunification requirements, 'and for us it goes hand in hand with the growth agenda. It needs to be made easier for people to come here if they want to contribute and if we need their competencies'.[34] 'With some people it is irrelevant whether they are much older than 24', said Prime Minister Lars Løkke Rasmussen on the new rule sys-tem, 'They simply shall not come in if they are only coming to be a burden to the Danish society'.[35] The Liberal Party's spokesperson for immigration and integration policy called the new family reunifica-tion points system 'the expression of a modern approach to society's development. Denmark should be an open but not a naive country'.[36]

The government and Danish People's Party worked to link the idea that even Danish citizens' choice of partner must be subsumed under considerations of national interest in a state struggling to compete on global markets, to the government and the Danish People's Party, with the economic crisis: 'At the same time, the economic crisis has changed the conditions in Denmark. It is fundamental that we realise this, and that we recognise that we face a common challenge. That is why those who receive spousal reunification in Denmark must contribute to the society's economy to a higher extent'.[37] Stricter rules for spousal reunification migrants and for all would-be immigrants were in this context necessary, said then-Integration Minister Birthe Rønn Hornbech, to contribute to 'growing the private sector and stopping the pressure on the public coffers'.[38]

Most controversially, in a late stage of the parliamentary debate on the law, the Minister for Integration Søren Pind introduced a further amendment whereby individuals from the USA, Canada, Australia, New Zealand, Japan and South Korea would be exempted from passing the immigration test as they applied for family reunification with Danish spouses. The suggestion was met with the above-mentioned concern over an alleged lack of substantial relevant grounds for differentiating requirements on the basis of applicants' national origin.

Non-economic arguments were also raised in favour of the stricter policies, highlighting the need to counter arranged marriages (to correct the loophole of waiting until after the age of 24), cultural/value distance and ease of integration, incentives and motivation concerns and access to Denmark being a gift which requires deservedness and commitment. Yet even the cultural adaptability, motivation and deservedness arguments were often linked to expected economic contribution.

These arguments did not go unchallenged, although the opposition was split. The small Social Liberal Party and the left-wing Red-Greens advocated an uncompromising cosmopolitan and individual rights-oriented stance against attempts to 'assign points to people's love', saying that 'it should be a fundamental right that you as a member of Danish society may fall in love with and marry a person from another country and then settle in Denmark'.[39] In parliament and in other public debates, the opposition appealed more clearly to Danes' right to freely establish family life than for already married couples to be allowed reunification, but in reality they sought changes to address both situations. For Marianne Jelved of the Social Liberal Party, the key concern was that 'Free personal choice and the right to a private life are very seriously violated by this law proposal'. Her party, she maintained, could not accept 'that permission for family reunification is determined by a points system that demands that the relationship between the applicant and the Danish-resident be evaluated on the basis of its value for desirable output as defined by a majority in Parliament'.[40]

The more hesitant Social Democratic and Socialist People's Parties, fearing electoral unease if cracks became visible in their recently adopted hard-line profile, proposed their own alternative, much less restrictive points system. At the same time, like the Social Liberal Party and the far left, they joined human rights scholars in criticising the discrimination and prejudice in the national origin-based exemptions and the bias towards privileged groups inherent in the high fees. Above all, they insisted on a distinction between a logic based on net benefit and economic growth and a more voluntaristic and moral willingness-to-belong logic. The two parties' immigration and integration spokespersons pinpointed this rhetorically in the double question: 'Should people who wish to migrate under family reunification to Denmark be evaluated on their contribution to the gross national product? Or should people be evaluated on their wish and will to become a part of Danish society? The Social Democrats and Socialist People's Party have no doubt on this'.[41]

Yet the Socialist People's Party also saw no problem in integration demands per se on family-reunified spouses saying that they indicate 'basic recognition and respect' and reflect the best interest of these individuals themselves, in that the demands involve their having basic language skills and employment potential before they come.[42] Indeed,

> What advantage does a woman have from, for example, standing without competencies, hidden away in a ghetto? It is only good to ask the applicant to prepare some foundational language skills in Danish or English, so they can get along in Denmark or for example be available for the labor market or education when they are in Denmark.[43]

Implicit in the socialists' viewpoint is the idea that a satisfying family life, in Denmark at least, requires women to work and earn their own income.

Welfare, Growth and Family Rights: The Growing International Framework

Immigrant-receiving states must continue to weigh individual family rights with the need to sustain the welfare state and economic growth. The Danish experiment with an extremely restrictive family reunification regime through the 2000s was chiefly driven by a desire to make all immigration, even family migration, profitable for the welfare society. Concerns over cultural integration contributed to the debates and policies, but economic arguments for restricting family reunification rights held increasing sway as the welfare state began to face deficits in an economic downturn. The results for family migration were mixed, however, and concerns about rights violations remained.

Ultimately, the subsequent government has chosen to repeal the deepest restrictions to family migration, mainly to answer the most pressing rights concerns. It will remove the most recent restrictions, including the points system for foreign-resident spouses and the requirement that a couple have *substantially stronger* ties to Denmark than any other country. The requirement for stronger ties will now be waived after the resident spouse has lived in the country for 26 years, rather than 28. Furthermore, recent increases in visa application fees and the size of bank guarantee required will be returned to previous levels, and the entering spouse will no longer be required to take an immigration exam within three months of arrival. The centre-left government has essentially promised to repeal the steepest, most recent restrictions and return the rules to what existed in 2009, but is not likely to undo the previous government's main family reunification policy changes.

Interestingly, Denmark's policies during this period revealed a growing potential paradox for family migration policy throughout Europe. Increasingly, international rights conventions limit state autonomy in legislating family migration rules regarding refugees, EU and candidate-country citizens, and even third-country nationals living within state territory. The first two groups are already extensively protected by the international charters and European law, and the rights of third-country nationals will need to be taken greater account of – in Denmark, especially if the country withdraws its exceptions to following EU policy, among them the immigration and integration area. If such developments continue, national states will only be able to legislate over reunification policy concerning their own citizens' relatives. This limitation will paradoxically be reinforced in countries that, like Denmark, raise significant barriers to immigrant naturalisation: since many migrants and their descendants are not eligible for citizenship, the national legislators may face scenarios in which the very people whose family reunification they most wish to influence are beyond their reach.

Notes

1. The authors would like to thank Kristian Jensen, PhD Student in Political Science, Aarhus University, for research assistance on this work.

2. Liisberg, M. V. 'Regler og administrative praksis for ægtefællesammenføring [Rules and Practice of Family Reunification]'. *Ægtefællesammenføring i Danmark: Udredning nr. 1* [Family Reunification in Denmark: Review no. 1]. Copenhagen: Danish Institute for Human Rights, 2004.

3. Introduced in Law 365, June 2002.

4. Liisberg: 'Regler og administrative praksis for ægtefællesammenføring [Rules and Practice of Family Reunification]'.

5. The support requirement could, however, be waived in 'quite special circumstances' such as for refugees who face perpetual persecution in their homelands and who seek reunification with a spouse to whom they were already married when they themselves entered Denmark, for handicapped individuals for whom such a requirement would violate international conventions, for some individuals with existing child-support obligations in Denmark, and for some students in the process of a competence-giving

education. Refugees still in danger of persecution in their countries of origin who were married to their spouses before entering Denmark may be exempted from several other requirements as well.

6. Danish Ministry for Refugees, Immigration and Integration. 'Forslag til Lov om ændring af udlændingeloven, Høringsudkast [Recommendation for: Law on change to the immigration law, Hearing Draft]'. Copenhagen, 3 February 2011.

7. Danish Ministry for Refugees, Immigration and Integration, 'Tal og faktaomintegration: Befolkning, uddannelse, beskæftigelse (Tema om born) [Numbers and facts about integration: Population, education, employment (Special issue on children)]'. Copenhagen, September 2010.

8. Schmidt, G., Liversage, A. Graversen, B. K., Jensen, T. G. and Jacobsen, V. *Ændrede familiesammenføringsregler: Hvad har de nye regler betydet for pardannelsesmønstret blant etniske minoriteter?* [Changed Family Reunification Rules: What have the new rules meant for partnership formation patternsamongethnic minorities?]. Copenhagen: SFI, 2009.

9. The rates of marriage to individuals living in another country differ for men and women: for men, the proportion fell from 68.1% in 2001 to 38.7% in 2009. For women, it fell from 52.2% in 2001 to 20.5% in 2009. Source: Danish Ministry for Refugees, Immigration and Integration: 'Tal og faktaomintegration: Befolkning, uddannelse, beskæftigelse (Tema om born) [Numbers and facts about integration: Population, education, employment (Special issue on children)]'. Copenhagen, September 2010.

10. Schmidt et al.: *Ændrede familiesammenfringsregler: Hvad har de nye regler betydet for pardannelsesmnstret blant etniske minoriteter?*

11. Øresundsbro konsortiet och Öresundskomiteen. 'Danska erfarenheter av att bo i Skåne [Danish Experiences of Living in Skåne]', 2005.

12. Hergel, O. and Albæk, M. 'Udlædinge med høj uddannelse føler sig afvist [Well-educated foreigners feel rejected]'. *Politiken*, 2 October 2010.

13. Danish Government and the Danish People's Party. *Aftale: Nye Tider. Nye Krav* [Agreement: New Times, New Requirements]. Copenhagen, 7 November 2010. http://www.danskfolkeparti. dk/pictures_org/nye_tider_nye_krav(1).pdf.

14. Danish Government and the Danish Peoples Party: *Aftale: Nye Tider. Nye Krav.*

15. Unless the foreign spouse is a citizen of Australia, Canada, Israel, Japan, New Zealand, Switzerland, South Korea or the United States. Turkish citizens are not required to pay the exam fee.

16. Davidsen-Nielsen, H. and Maltesen, B. 'Færre søger om at få familien til Danmark [Fewer apply to get their families into Denmark]'. *Politiken*, 21 June 2011.

17. Cited in Davidsen-Nielsen and Maltesen: 'Færre søger om at få familien til Danmark [Fewer apply to get their families into Denmark]'.

18. Council of Europe, Art. 8, par. 1–2.

19. Danish Institute for Human Rights (DIHR). 'Bemærkninger: Hring over udkast til forslag til lov om ændring af udlændingeloven (reform af gtefællesammenføringsreglerne m.v.), p. 5 [Comments: Hearing on Proposed Bill Draft for a Law for Changing the Aliens Act/Immigration Law/ (Reform of Spousal Reunification Rules, etc.)]'. J.nr 10/27352. Copenhagen, 10 March 2011. J.Nr.540.10/24801/SWG.

20. Danish Institute for Human Rights (DIHR): 'Bemærkninger: Høring over udkast til forslag til lov om ændring af udlændingeloven (reform af gtefællesammenføringsreglerne m.v.), p. 6.

21. Danish Institute for Human Rights (DIHR): 'Bemærkninger: Høring over udkast til forslag til lov om ændring af udlændingeloven (reform af gtefællesammenføringsreglerne m.v.), ref. to United Nations. International Convention on the Elimination of All Forms of Racial Discrimination. 21 December 1965; United Nations. Convention on the Elimination of All Forms of Discrimination against Women. 18 December 1979; and United Nations (2006). Convention on the Rights of Persons with Disabiliities. 13 December 2006.

22. Danish Institute for Human Rights (DIHR): 'Bemærkninger: Høring over udkast til forslag til lov om ændring af udlændingeloven (reform af gtefællesammenføringsreglerne m.v.)', pp. 8, 23.

23. Danish Institute for Human Rights (DIHR): 'Bemærkninger: Høring over udkast til forslag til lov om ændring af udlændingeloven (reform af gtefællesammenføringsreglerne m.v.)'.

24. Danish Institute for Human Rights (DIHR): 'Bemærkninger: Høring over udkast til forslag til lov om ændring af udlændingeloven (reform af gtefællesammenføringsreglerne m.v.)', pp. 13–14.

25. Danish Institute for Human Rights (DIHR): 'Bemærkninger: Høring over udkast til forslag til lov om ændring af udlændingeloven (reform af gtefællesammenføringsreglerne m.v.)', p. 15, referring to national law precedent when considering other immigration policies.

26. Brochman, G. and Hagelund, A. *Velferdens grenser* [Welfare's borders]. Oslo: Universitetsforlaget, 2010.

27. Mouritsen, P. and Olsen, T. V. 'Denmark Between Liberalism and Nationalism'. *Ethnic and Racial Studies* (2012). http://www.tandfonline.com/doi/abs/10.1080/01419870.2011.598233; Jensen, M. U. *Et delt Folk* [A divided people]. Odense: Lysias (2008).

28. Hvenegaard-Lassen, K. *På lige fod, samfundet, ligheden og folketingets debatter om udlændingepolitik 1973–2000* [On equal footing: society, equality and Parliament's debates over immigration policy 1973–2000], PhD dissertation, Faculty of Humanities, Copenhagen University, Copenhagen, Denmark, 2002.

29. Integration Law, article 1.

30. For instance, since 2003 individual immigrants must repay the 'introductory payments' they have received if they have not participated in the introduction programme, and more recently earlier permanent residence has been made possible for people with better labour-market participation records; Clemmesen, C. S. 'Noget for noget – Diskursivt sceneskift i velfaerdsstaten!' Roskilde

Universitetscenter 2005, pp. 50–1. http://rudar.ruc.dk/bitstream/ 1800/763/1/Carolines%20Speciale%20Kopi.pdf.

31. For details, see Mouritsen, P. 'Beyond Post-national Citizenship: Access, Consequence, Conditionality'. In A. Triandafyllidou, T. Modood and N. Meer (eds) *European Multiculturalisms: Cultural, Religious and Ethnic Challenges*. Edinburgh: Edinburgh University Press, 2011.

32. Wadensjö, E. and Orrje, H. *Immigration and the Public Sector in Denmark*. Aarhus: Aarhus University Press (2002).

33. Minister of Integration Søren Pind presentation of law no. L 168 2010–11, https://www.retsinformation.dk/Forms/R0710.aspx?id =136290.

34. Naser Khader, cited in Jessen, C. K. and Thobo-Carlsen, J. 'Dansk Folkeparti: Nogle skal slet ikke have familiesammenføring'. *Berlingske Tidende*, 6 November 2010.

35. Rasmussen, L. L. *Speech at the Liberal Party Annual Party Meeting*, 2010, p. 10. http://www.venstre.dk/fileadmin/user upload/Taler/ llrlandsmoede2010.pdf. Tilgået 09.09.2011.

36. MP Karsten Lauritzen, remark during first reading of L 168 2010–11. http://www.ft.dk/samling/20101/lovforslag/l168/beh1/ 2/forhandling.htm?startItem=#nav.

37. Danish Government and the Danish Peoples Party: *Aftale: Nye Tider. Nye Krav.*

38. Hornbech, B. R. 'Krisen baner nye veje i udlændingepolitikken [The crisis is paving new ways in immigration policy]'. *Berlingske Tidende*, 9 November 2010.

39. Parliamentary debate on law no. L 168 2010–11. 'Forslag til lov om ændring af udlændingeloven og lov om ægteskabs indgæelse og opløsning (Reform af ægtefællesammenføringsreglerne m.v.) [Proposal for a law on changing the immigration law and the law on entry into and dissolution of marriage (Reform of family migration rules, etc.)]'.

40. Jelved, M. Speech delivered at the first reading of law no. L 168 2010–11 (1.samling). http://www.ft.dk/samling/20101/lovforslag/ L168/BEH1/ forhandling.htm#dok, 2010.

41. Kristensen, H. D. and Krag, A. 'Folk skal vurderes på viljen til integration – ikke nytteværdi [People should be evaluated on their will to integrate – not their profitability]'. *Politiken,* 21 November 2010.

42. MP Astrid Krag, remark during first reading of law no. L 168 2010–11. http://www.ft.dk/samling/20101/lovforslag/l168/beh1/88/forhandling.htm?startItem=#nav.

43. Kristensen and Krag: 'Folk skal vurderes på viljen til integration – ikke nytteværdi [People should be evaluated on their will to integrate – not their profitability]'.

Further Reading

Council of Europe. 'Convention for the Protection of Human Rights and Fundamental Freedoms'. Rome, 4 November 1950. http://conventions.coe.int/Treaty/Commun/QueVoulezVous.asp?NT=005&CM=8&DF=07/10/2011&CL=ENG.

Danish Government and the Danish People's Party. *Udlændingeaftale* [Immigration Agreement]. Copenhagen, 6 November 2009.

Danish Government and the Danish People's Party. *Aftale: Ny regler for at få permanent opholdstilladelse og serviceeftersyn af udlændinge- og integrationspolitikken* [Agreement: New Rules for Getting Permanent Residency and Tune-up of Immigration and Integration Policy]. Copenhagen, 15 March 2010.

CHAPTER 10

Migration, Immigration Controls and the Fashioning of Precarious Workers

Bridget Anderson

Immigration controls are often presented by government as a means of ensuring 'British jobs for British workers' and protecting migrants from exploitation. Concern for both the displacement of British workers and the exploitation of foreign labour stems from the common image of migrants working at the sharp end of de-regulated labour markets in jobs characterised by low wages, insecurity and murky employment relations.[1] The explanations for migrant concentration in these sectors tend to focus on discrimination, poor language knowledge, illegality and a lack of recognition of qualifications, all set against the backdrop of global inequality which incentivises some migrants to take on jobs at wages and conditions that many UK nationals would not consider.

The extent to which the UK immigration regime itself undermines the national labour force in employment and makes migrants vulnerable to exploitation and abuse is, however, often overlooked. This chapter will argue that immigration controls, often characterised as a tap regulating the flow of workers, can also be seen to function as a mould that forms particular relations between employers and workers. The conditions of institutionalised uncertainty that the immigration system imposes on migrants work in combination with informal migratory processes to help produce 'precarious workers' over whom employers and labour workers have particular mechanisms of control.

Recent Developments in Immigration Rhetoric, Policy and Controls

Considerable attention has recently been paid to migrants in low waged, often abusive employment.[2] This concern has been raised outside the 'usual suspects' of migration scholars and activists – many of whom would contend that there is nothing new about the abuse and misuse of migrant labour – and includes the UK Home Office:

> Failure to take on the people traffickers . . . leaves vulnerable and often desperate people at the mercy of organized criminals. But equally importantly, the fact that many immigrants, at the end of their journey, end up in shadowy jobs in the grey economy undermines the terms and working conditions of British workers. That's not fair . . . We have to tackle not only the illegal trafficked journeys but also the illegal jobs at the end of them.[3]

Thus, both the poor working conditions of migrant labour and the competition faced by British workers and businesses are attributed to aberrations in the labour market ('grey economy') and in the immigration system ('illegality'), indicating the need for immigration controls and enforcement. A rare coincidence of interest is indicated between government and those concerned with migrant exploitation and abuse, both determined to stamp out 'trafficking'. Immigration controls are presented here as an integral part of a restructured immigration system which aims to facilitate legitimate travel and trade; ensures security from crime, terrorism and 'attacks on the tax base'; and protects the border as well as 'providing reassurance for the general public and business'.[4]

Thus, on 29 February 2008, a new civil penalty scheme for employers came into force. Under this scheme an employer faces fines of up to £10,000 per illegal worker. A maximum sentence of two years was also introduced for the new criminal offence of *knowingly* employing an illegal worker. The names of employers so convicted or subject to civil penalties are published on a monthly basis.

The implementation of the Australian-style 'points-based system' in 2008 was furthermore affected by the earlier introduction of ten new countries to the European Union in May 2004, including the 'Accession 8' or A8 states, predominantly of Eastern Europe. A8 nationals could take up employment in the UK without restriction as long as they registered with the Worker Registration Scheme (WRS). The numbers of A8 nationals who came to the UK to work significantly exceeded government expectations. Therefore, while the new system allowed for several categories of immigrants, Tier 3 (low-skilled workers) began as an 'empty category', with Tier 2 (skilled) representing the only means of general labour recruitment to the UK from outside the EU.

Migration and 'Precarity'

It has long been recognised that the migration of people into low-wage 'precarious' labour, as an economic phenomenon and as a social process, is related to wider global factors.[5] Examples include the role of guestworker schemes in migration, increasingly inserted into more general debates about 'precarious workers' particularly in Italy, Spain and France.[6]

The notion of 'precarity' captures both atypical and insecure employment and has implications beyond employment pointing to an associated weakening of social relations and focus on economic productivity. In this sense precarious work results in *precarité*, a more general concern with precariousness of life which prevents people from anticipating the future.[7] Thus, precarity foregrounds the temporal and spatial aspects of work and migration.[8] The 'illegal' migrant who, as Ahmad strikingly puts it, is 'living off borrowed time' has become emblematic of the 'precarious worker'.[9] These temporal aspects are manifest in immigration controls (the time dimensions of immigration programmes are crucial to their workings), as well as the nature and type of employment that migrants find.

Certain stages of migration, when it is viewed as a dynamic, temporal process, clearly interact with the temporal requirements of certain types of labour markets. Take agency working for example. The UK has the largest penetration of agency workers in the European Union (4.2 per cent) and in January 2008, 58 per cent of Jobcentre Plus vacancies were for 'other business activities', largely comprised of employment agency vacancies.[10] This finding puts the demand 'British jobs for British workers' in a new light, and goes some way toward explaining the claim that 52 per cent of jobs go to 'new migrants'. Some 25 per cent of agency workers in the UK are migrants,[11] often working in specific sectors – one study found that 90 per cent of agency workers employed in second stage food processing were migrants.[12]

There are many qualitative studies detailing migrants' situations in what might be termed precarious employment, but large-scale data are weak.[13] However, Labour Force Survey (LFS) data suggest that recent migrants (defined in October 2008 as those who arrived between October 1997 and October 2007) are more than twice as likely as UK nationals to be in temporary work, and there are good reasons for believing that these data represent a significant underestimation.[14] Whatever the scepticism about the extent of insecure work, migrants are disproportionately concentrated in it.[15]

Precarity and Migratory Processes

Piore argues that the imagined temporariness of new migrants' stay means that more recent migrants, perhaps with lower subjective expectations, less language and a more limited understanding of the labour market, are more likely to view work purely instrumentally in terms of temporary benefit rather than as a 'job for life'.[16] They may envisage staying only for a limited period, or may plan to move to better things, perhaps when their language has improved, and/or when they have better contacts or accommodation possibilities. Whether as an opportunity to get a foot on the ladder or to learn English, or to repay debt incurred as part of the migratory process, precarious work may be work to which the temporary migrant as 'true economic man' is particularly suited.[17]

The current position of A8 nationals in the UK labour market is recognisably 'Piorean'. WRS data indicate that recent A8 arrivals are predominantly employed in low-waged work. Of those who had registered between October 2006 and September 2007, 8.8 per cent were earning below the adult minimum wage of £5.35 an hour (since these figures do not allow for the accommodation offset, the figures can serve as a benchmark only). According to WRS data the 10 occupations that were the largest employers of A8 migrants between July 2004 to March 2009 were all 'low skilled', the largest group being 'process operatives (other factory worker)', which accounted for 28 per cent of all registrations.[18] Ninety-six per cent were working 'full time', defined as 16 hours or more a week, and including multiple job holding.

With insecurity often comes long or short and/or anti-social hours. The expectation of a temporary stay can result in a lack of social attachment and a preparedness to forego social pleasures. Households may be simply temporary accommodation arrangements rather than social units. Moreover, as Nicole-Drancourt argues, those who are young are more likely to tolerate flexibility and unpredictability, meaning recently arrived migrants have a much younger age profile compared to the established population: according to the LFS, among those arriving in the UK between 1997 and 2007, around four fifths were between the ages of 16 and 40, compared to two fifths in the entire sample.[19]

The concentration of migrants (including legal residents who do not yet have permanent stay) in precarious work is in part the result of migratory processes (which are of course themselves functions of other kinds of processes including employers' targeted recruitment). However, as people 'develop a more permanent attachment, their time horizon expands and in particular instability of employment is no longer a matter of indifference.'[20] Employers who extol the virtues of migrants are thus often specifically thinking of recent arrivals (a nuance that is lost through the use of the definition 'foreign born'). Piore argues that this development is related to the construction of and participation in community, but it is also crucially related to legal status. European Union citizens are a Piorean case study, but importantly their temporariness is not state-enforceable and their time horizon may indeed expand. In contrast, the citizens of many non-EU member states are likely to find the development of 'permanent attachment' obstructed or downright prevented by immigration controls and citizenship legislation.

Denaturalising Immigration Controls

Immigration controls reinforce some temporal aspects of migratory processes (the initial assumption of temporariness within some groups of migrants) and may undermine others (including a disposition to settlement). In most liberal democracies', length of stay has implications for rights-based claims and certain groups can progress from temporary, to settled status and thence to citizenship.[21] In this way, Piore's explanation of migrants' positions in secondary labour markets can be refined by relating differential labour-market positions to the workings of immigration controls.

Immigration controls work with and against migratory processes to produce workers with particular relations to employers and to labour markets. The impact of illegality and its relation to 'exploitation' have received considerable attention.[22] However, illegality has tended to be theorised as *absence* of legal status (and therefore of access to state protection), rather than as immigration controls 'producing' illegality.[23] Such insights need to be developed into an examination of how immigration controls produce status more generally, in order to analyse the types of *legality* so produced and the impact of these on migrants' positions in labour markets.[24]

The way in which immigration controls produce status can roughly be divided into three: the creation of categories of entrant, the influencing of employment relations and the institutionalisation of uncertainty. It is important to note from the outset that state enforcement of these regulations (i.e. not only deportation but also bureaucratic controls over immigration status and access to employment) is relatively well resourced. Compare the projected costs for the enforcement of the National Minimum Wage (NMW) in 2009/10 at £8.8 million, with the budget for the UK border force (not including Customs Detection activity funding) for the same period at £248.6 million.[25] The budget for in-country immigration control (work permits, points-based system, removals, asylum processes) was £884.3 million.[26]

The Creation of Categories of Entrant

Immigration controls are typically presented as a filter, allowing in the skilled, students, those with family ties, tourists and other legitimate groups like au pairs, while filtering out undesirables including criminals and those without the skills to benefit the economy. In this rather narrow sense the role of immigration controls in constructing a labour force is broadly recognised. The government argues that the points-based system offers greater flexibility for accommodating new economic circumstances. Thus in February 2009 then-Home Secretary Jacqui Smith increased the minimum qualification for Tier 1 from a BA to a Master's degree, and the minimum salary from £17,000 to £20,000 a year. She stated on BBC television: 'Just as in a growth period we needed migrants to support growth, it is right in a downturn to be more selective about the skill levels of those migrants, and to do more to put British workers first'.[27]

However, one does not have to be a Tier 1 or 2 applicant to enter under the PBS at all, in order to participate legally in the labour market. Students, for instance, may work 20 hours in term time and 40 hours a week in the holidays; working holidaymakers may work for up to 12 months of their allotted two-year stay. In 2005, 91,500 work permits were granted, 284,000 students were given leave to enter and there were 56,600 working holidaymakers, but only the first of these 'count' as workers.[28]

However, it is not only skills, earnings and experience that shape categories of entrant, but age, country of origin and in some instances marital status. The additional 20 points awarded to Tier 1 workers under the age of 28 aim to correct an inherent bias against younger workers in a system that awards points on the basis of earnings and level of qualifications (both of which are likely to increase with age).

Thus, immigration controls are being used to shape and reinforce those aspects of migratory processes that mean that migrants are likely to have a younger age profile. They may also reinforce what Piore calls the 'plasticity' of the work force.[29] Just because a visa category effectively 'permits' the applicant to be married or have children does not mean that the spouse or children are eligible to enter the UK, or to have recourse to public funds (including housing); so, for many migrants subject to immigration control, household commitments are more limited than they are for other low-waged workers, which can mean some are more likely to work longer days and through weekends.[30] The settlement process whereby migrants become embedded in social and other networks outside of work may further be artificially halted by immigration and citizenship requirements.

Under the UK system, only Tiers 1 and 2 can lead to permanent settlement, and in April 2012 it was announced that Tier 2 workers' access to settlement would be substantially limited.

The Moulding of Employment Relations

Immigration controls are not a neutral framework facilitating the sorting of individuals by intentions and identities into particular categories, rather they *produce status* and the type of visa obtained often has important and long-term effects on where migrants work in the labour market. Take for example the role of A8 nationals in the construction industry. The importance of this group of migrants in this sector needs to be seen within the context of the prevalence of 'false self employment' in construction. In the 1990s so-called Association Agreements allowed nationals from states that were going to join the EU to enter the UK as effectively 'own account self employed' without the large capital sum required of other nationalities. Those who entered under such arrangements were not necessarily budding entrepreneurs; rather, self employment was, for certain nationals, particularly men, one of the easiest ways to enter the UK and work legally. It is scarcely surprising that many of those holding self-employment visas gravitated to the construction sector, where this form of self employment proliferated. Migration scholars, such as Massey, have demonstrated that networks of employment and immigration have their own dynamic over time. Once networks have become entrenched in particular sectors they may continue to function even if the legislative framework shifts.[31]

Immigration controls are not simply about conditions of entry across the border, but about conditions of stay. Once non-citizens have entered the UK (legally), they are subject to particular conditions depending on their visa status. Most non-citizens who are admitted to work have their access to the labour market limited in some way. Migrants must have a 'certificate of sponsorship' from their employer. An employer may withdraw the certificate of sponsorship at any time and the migrant will have to leave the UK within 60 days if they have not found another authorised sponsor (the certificate may be withdrawn immediately if the Home Office believes it was issued improperly).

Thus, many workers subject to immigration control are effectively on fixed-term contracts that may be terminated at the employer's discretion, producing a temporariness that, unlike the temporariness of A8 nationals, for instance, can be enforced by the state through removal from UK territory. To this extent, legal migrants on work-related visas are dependent on the goodwill of their employer for their right to remain in the UK, and are therefore also 'precarious workers'. The new system has not yet been tested, but under the old system permits could be given for up to five years (after which a non-citizen may apply for settlement), but immigration instructions favoured shorter periods. In 2005, out of 91,500 work permits, 40,300 were given for fewer than 12 months.[32] Renewals must be supported by the employer, and in the same year there were 68,980 applications for work permit extensions.[33] It is worth observing that if the worker's salary had 'significantly' increased since the initial application, that is above annual increments, the extension was not automatically granted, as it was argued that UK/EU nationals may be more interested in applying for the job. The combination of temporariness and labour-market immobility, both pre-requisites of the work permit system and sponsorship arrangements, reinforced migrants' dependence on employers.

Not only is the employment mobility of migrants on work permits limited by the state, but employers are handed additional means of control: for any reason or, indeed, even a personal grudge, not only the worker's job, but their residency, can be put in jeopardy. Thus, compliant workers can feel unable to challenge employers and in some instances employers have taken advantage of immigration status as a means of exercising control over work-permit holders, including forbidding union membership. No claims can be made for the extent of such practices, but those on work permits may be conscious enough of this possibility to police themselves. In this way, workers who are subject to immigration controls may be more desirable to employers than those (migrants and citizens) who are not.[34]

The work permit/sponsorship system means that employers have powers of labour retention without jeopardising their ability to fire (though hiring may indeed be more cumbersome). When asked why they employ migrants, employers have been found to frequently refer to *retention* as an advantage of migrant labour.[35] Other perceived advantages, often racialised by employers, such as reliability, honesty and work ethic must also be understood partly in terms of the level of dependence work permit holders have on their employers.[36] Moreover, while labour mobility tends to be thought of as a particular problem for the employers who require 'skilled' work, government restrictions on schemes for the entrance of 'low-skilled' workers have received particular criticism because of their impact on retention. The National Farmers Union, for example, has been vocal in its opposition to the shrinking of the Seasonal Agricultural Workers Scheme (SAWS), which only allows visa holders to move their employment to another registered farm. Agricultural employers themselves acknowledge that there are practical difficulties with finding new employers in rural areas and often described SAWS workers as 'tied' by their permit.

> Migrant workers are an attractive source of labour to UK employers because of their work ethos, efficiency and dependency and because, particularly in the case of the SAWS, they provide a source of labour that is guaranteed to remain on farm during the crucial harvest period.[37]

However, not all employers value retention over flexibility. The work-permit scheme requires employers to submit documentation within tight deadlines, to anticipate demand and to take on employment responsibilities, in some instances even accommodation, for workers. They risk tying themselves into obligations that are not necessarily profitable, and turn instead to labour already in the UK. These workers may or may not be UK nationals, but if they are not, they are rarely work permit holders and are not necessarily entrants on schemes. It is here the imagined distinction between 'migrant worker' and migration for other purposes starts to break down, held together only by the administrative rules and practices that claim to describe rather than form them.[38] Groups that may work without being restricted to named employers or sectors include holidaymakers and students, for whom restrictions on time are nonetheless important, limiting them to part-time or temporary work.

The Production of Institutionalised Uncertainty

Immigration law and practice are key to the creation of legality and its obverse. Borders are commonly perceived as keeping 'illegal immigrants' out, but migrants are not 'illegal' until they have crossed the border (or have attempted to do so), and very often not until well after that. Illegality is 'produced' by state laws and policies, for with selection and rules come exceptions, rule breakers, grey areas.[39] The construction of a category of people who are residing illegally is in part an inevitable function of any form of immigration control and nation state organised citizenship. The contradiction is, therefore, that in a bureaucratic and inevitably complex system of control, the state may perversely lose control over migration by creating greater numbers of over-stayers, people working in breach of conditions and illegal entrants.

Those workers who are 'illegal' are generally recognised to be highly vulnerable to exploitation and abuse as employers can use their lack of legal status to threaten and control them, and in practice they may be grossly over-dependent on their employer. The contradiction between state condemnation of such 'abuse of vulnerability' and state enforcement of employers' threat has not been challenged. Indeed, the figure of the abusive employer throws a shadow over the role of the state in constructing vulnerability. For example, while an abusive employer may deny basic employment rights to migrants who are working illegally, this denial of rights is legitimated through the doctrine of illegality which holds that a person should not profit from their wrongdoing. Thus, even if they have an employment contract, it cannot be enforced, and neither can any statutory rights, nor indeed statutory protection against discrimination.[40] Precarious work for those working illegally is not simply at the whim of individual employers, but structurally produced by the interaction of employment and immigration legislation.

As the government makes the lives of those working illegally 'ever more uncomfortable and constrained', so the predisposition to precarity increases. Rather than the pantomime 'evil employer', it is institutionalised uncertainty, again enforced by the state, that is the more mundane reality for many of those working illegally. The problem for them is not simply the risk of employer abuse, but enforced temporariness and the manner in which fear of deportation can lead to a pressure to maximise the 'now', whatever the current opportunities might be.[41] The extent to which deportability constrains is in part to do with individual psychology and circumstances, but state policy is deeply implicated.

The average cost of deportation is estimated by the National Audit Office at £11,000 per person, making the cost of deporting the estimated number of over-stayers £5.5 billion. Deportations are in practice targeted, with over-stayers who are young, educated and from countries with a high GDP imagined as unlikely to cause the kind of 'harm' that is likely from those from poorer countries who might go on to 'make an unfounded asylum claim'.[42] The available data on employers served with civil penalties for employing migrants lacking a right to employment is suggestive. Caution must be exercised in making assumptions, but it is notable that, to take a month selected at random, of the 126 employers listed in October 2008, the names of 112 of these suggest they might be first or second generation non-EU migrants.

Conclusions

The interaction between labour markets and immigration has been considerably researched and theorised, but research has tended to focus on 'illegality' on the one hand, and migratory processes on the other. Immigration controls come to the fore in discussions around 'trafficking' and illegality as a key explanatory variable for understanding migrants' vulnerability to poor employment. However, this approach means the problem then becomes bad employers, and the role of the state in illegalising workers is passed over. This chapter has argued for the importance of paying close attention to the relation between labour markets and immigration controls, which not only illegalise some groups but legalise others in very particular ways. In practice, as well as a tap regulating the flow of workers to a state, immigration controls might be more usefully conceived as a mould *constructing* certain types of workers through selection of legal entrants, the requiring and enforcing of certain types of employment relations, and the creation of institutionalised uncertainty.

Immigration controls effectively subject workers to a high degree of regulation, giving employers mechanisms of control that they do not have over citizens. This means that for certain (often very specific) occupations, immigration controls may not function as a means of protecting jobs for citizens but effectively create a group of workers that are *more desirable* as employees through enforcing atypical employment relations such as fixed-term contracts (and self employment) and direct dependence on employers for legal status. It is in this context that employers praise migrants' 'reliability' and call for an increase in numbers even at time of high unemployment. Thus, while 'illegality' is acknowledged as producing vulnerability to exploitation, this chapter argues that this is not, as commonly imagined, because of *absence* of status, but is an instance of one of the many ways in which immigration controls and migratory processes produce certain types of labour, including precarious workers. It is not only the smuggled 'illegal' worker who finds that 'the meaning of their existence . . . inheres exclusively in other times and places', but often 'legal' workers too.[43]

Of course, not all migrants are subject to immigration control. Migratory processes help provide a source of labour (often over-qualified) that is prepared to tolerate low-waged and insecure work, at least for a short time. Thus, A8 nationals often demonstrate the expectation of 'non-enforced' temporariness: workers who, for a variety of reasons, are imagined as likely to be temporary, but without the possibility of this temporariness being enforced through immigration controls. This raises the question of what happens when the immediate apparent coincidence of interests between employer and worker dissolves.[44] Yet in understanding the impact of migratory processes on the lives of migrants, we should not underestimate the importance of discrimination, lack of recognition of qualifications and education, and other 'demand' side factors in preventing people from moving out of low-waged, low-status and insecure jobs many years after they have obtained British citizenship.[45]

Some protections for precarious or vulnerable workers are unavailable in law to migrants. This is most obviously the case for those who are working in breach of immigration controls, but there are also instances when those who are working legally are nevertheless unprotected. The current Equalities Legislation specifically exempts those who are subject to immigration controls from local authorities' requirement to have due regard to socio-economic inequalities. If available, protections are typically difficult to access in practice because of the dependence on employers, which is actively enhanced by immigration controls. Immigration controls are not a means of protecting migrants' employment rights, but rather produce uncertainty and dependence on the employer, not just for work but often for legal or at least continuing residence in the UK. The extension of employment protection irrespective of immigration enforcement matters would be an important step in protecting the rights of migrant workers and potential undermining of employment standards and rights. At the same time, the situation of low-waged precarious migrant workers must be analysed within the context, not simply of abusive employers, but of the labour markets within which they work. Concerns about the impact of immigration on 'British workers' may ultimately be a conjuring trick, a masterpiece of public misdirection, when what merits attention are issues of job quality, job security and low pay. Immigration restriction and enforcement are not only insufficient to reduce migrant precarity, but actively produce and reinforce it.

Notes

1. May, J., Wills, J., Datta, K., Evans, Y., Herbert, J. and McIlwaine, C. *The British State and London's Migrant Division of Labour*. London: Queen Mary, University of London, 2006; Shelley, T. *Exploited: Migrant Labour in the New Global Economy*. London: Zed, 2007; TUC Commission on Vulnerable Employment. *Hard Work, Hidden Lives: The Full Report of the Commission on Vulnerable Employment*. London: Trades Union Congress, 2008.

2. Rogaly, B. 'Migrant Workers in the ILO's "Global Alliance Against Forced Labour" Report: A Critique'. *Third World Quarterly*, 29/7

(2008): 1431–47; TUC Commission on Vulnerable Employment: *Hard Work, Hidden Lives: The Full Report of the Commission on Vulnerable Employment.*

3. John Reid, MP, in Home Office. *Enforcing the Rules: A Strategy to Ensure and Enforce Compliance With Our Immigration Laws.* London: COI, 2007, p. 2.

4. Cabinet Office. *Security in a Global Hub: Establishing the UK's New Border Arrangements.* London: HMSO, 2007, p. 9.

5. Balibar, E. *We, the People of Europe? Reflections on Transnational Citizenship.* Princeton: Princeton University Press, 2004; Hardt, M. and Negri, A. *Empire.* Cambridge, MA: Harvard University Press, 2000; Sassen, S. *The Mobility of Labour and Capital: A Study in International Investment and Labour Flows.* Cambridge: Cambridge University Press, 1988.

6. Fantone, L. 'Precarious Changes: Gender and Generational Politics in Contemporary Italy'. *Feminist Review,* 87 (2007): 5–20; Papadopoulos, D., Stephenson, N. and Tsianos, V. *Escape Routes: Control and Subversion in the 21st Century.* London: Pluto Press, 2008.

7. Barbier, J.-C., Brygoo, A. and Viguier, F. *Defining and Assessing Precarious Employment in Europe: A Review of Main Studies and Surveys, a Tentative Approach to Precarious Employment in France.* Paris: Centre d'etude de l'emploi, 2002.

8. Cwerner, S. 'The Times of Migration'. *Journal of Ethnic and Migration Studies,* 27/1 (2001): 7–36.

9. Ahmad, A. 'Dead Men Working: Time and Space in London's (illegal) Migrant Economy'. *Work, Employment and Society,* 22/2 (2008): 301–18.

10. TUC Commission on Vulnerable Employment: *Hard Work, Hidden Lives: The Full Report of the Commission on Vulnerable Employment.*

11. Vosko, L. F. 'Less Than "Adequate": Regulating Temporary Agency Work in the EU in the Face of a Free Market in Services'. In *Transforming Work.* St John's College, Oxford, September 2008.

12. Geddes, A. *Staff Shortages and Immigration in Food Processing: A Report Prepared for the Migration Advisory Committee*. London: Migration Advisory Committee, 2008.

13. Ahmad: 'Dead Men Working: Time and Space in London's (illegal) Migrant Economy'; May et al.: *The British State and London's Migrant Division of Labour*; Pai, H-H. *Chinese Whispers: The True Story Behind Britain's Hidden Army of Labour*. London: Penguin Books, 2008; House of Lords. *The Economic Impact of Immigration*. London: The Stationery Office Limited, 2008.

14. Jayaweera, H. and Anderson, B. *Migrant Workers and Vulnerable Employment: A Review of Existing Data*. London: Trades Union Congress, 2008.

15. Fevre, R. 'Employment Insecurity and Social Theory: The Power of Nightmares'. *Work, Employment and Society*, 21/3 (2007): 517–35.

16. Piore, M. J. *Birds of Passage: Migrant Labour and Industrial Societies*. Cambridge: Cambridge University Press, 1979; Curtis, S. and Lucas, R. 'A Coincidence of Needs? Employers and Full-Time Students'. *Employee Relations*, 23/1 (2001): 38–54.

17. Piore: *Birds of Passage: Migrant Labour and Industrial Societies*, p. 54.

18. UK Border Agency. *Accession Monitoring Report, May 2004– December 2008*, http://www.ukba.homeoffice.gov.uk/sitecontent/documents/aboutus/reports/_accession_monitoring_report, p. 15.

19. Nicole-Drancourt, C. 'L'idée de précarité revisitée'. *Travail et Emploi*, 52 (1992): 57–70; Jayaweera and Anderson: *Migrant Workers and Vulnerable Employment: A Review of Existing Data*.

20. Piore: *Birds of Passage: Migrant Labour and Industrial Societies*, p. 64.

21. Carens, J. 'Live-In Domestics, Seasonal Workers, Foreign Students and Others Hard to Locate on the Map of Democracy'. In *Borders, Migrant Agency and the State: Surveying the Ethics of Borders from Disciplinary Borderland*. Centre on Migration, Policy

and Society, University of Oxford, 2007; Cole, P. *Philosophies of Exclusion: Liberal Political Theory and Immigration.* Edinburgh: Edinburgh University Press, 2000.

22. See Wright, T. and McKay, S. *United Kingdom Country Report.* London: Working Lives Research Institute, 2007, for a review.

23. De Genova, N. 'Migrant "Illegality" and Deportability in Everyday Life'. *Annual Review of Anthropology,* 31 (2002): 419–47.

24. Bauder, H. *Labor Movement: How Migration Regulates Labor Markets.* Oxford: Oxford University Press, 2006.

25. UK Border Agency Business Plan April 2009–March 2012.

26. UK Border Agency Business Plan April 2009–March 2012.

27. Cited in Rogers, A. *Recession, Vulnerable Workers and Immigration: A Background Report.* Oxford: Centre on Migration, Policy and Society, 2009.

28. Their spouses, who are unrestricted in the labour market as long as they continue to be a spouse, are defined as 'dependants'.

29. Piore: *Birds of Passage: Migrant Labour and Industrial Societies.*

30. Preibisch, K. and Binford, L. 'Interrogating Racialized Global Labour Supply: An Exploration of the Racial/National Replacement of Foreign Agricultural Workers'. *The Canadian Review of Sociology and Anthropology/LaRevue Canadienne de Sociologie et d'Anthropologie,* 44/1 (2007): 5–36.

31. Massey, D. S. 'Social Structure, Household Strategies, and the Cumulative Causation of Migration'. *Population Index,* 56/1 (1990): 3–26.

32. Of these, approximately 15,000 would have been SBS permits and therefore not eligible for extension.

33. Home Office. *Control of Immigration Statistics 2005.* Command Paper CM 6904. London: COI, 2005.

34. Rosenhek, Z. 'The Political Dynamics of a Segmented Labour Market: Palestinian Citizens, Palestinians from the Occupied Territories and Migrant Workers in Israel'. *Acta Sociologica,* 46/3(2003): 231–49.

35. Dench, S., Hurstfield, J., Hill, D. and Akroyd, K. *Employers' Use of Migrant Labour*. Home Office Online Report 04/06 (2006) http://www.homeoffice.gov.uk/rds/pdfs06/rdsolr0406.pdf; Waldinger, R. D. and Lichter, M. *How the Other Half Works: Immigration and the Social Organization of Labor*. Berkeley: University of California Press, 2003.

36. Gordon, J. and Lenhardt, R. A. 'Rethinking Work and Citizenship'. *UCLA Law Review*, 55 (2008): 1161–238.

37. House of Lords: *The Economic Impact of Immigration*, p. 100.

38. King, R. 'Towards a New Map of European Migration'. *International Journal of Population Geography*, 8/2 (2002): 89–106.

39. Black, R. 'Breaking the Convention: Researching the "Illegal" Migration of Refugees to Europe'. *Antipode*, 35 (2003): 35–54.

40. Ryan, B. 'The Evolving Legal Regime on Unauthorized Work by Migrants in Britain'. *Comparative Labor Law and Policy Journal*, 27 (2005): 27–58.

41. Ahmad: 'Dead Men Working: Time and Space in London's (illegal) Migrant Economy.'

42. Home Office. *Enforcing the Rules: A Strategy to Ensure and Enforce Compliance With Our Immigration Laws*. London: COI, 2007.

43. Ahmad: 'Dead Men Working: Time and Space in London's (illegal) Migrant Economy', p. 315.

44. Mackenzie, R. and Forde, C. 'The Rhetoric of the "Good Worker" Versus the Realities of Employers' Use and the Experiences of Migrant Workers'. *Work, Employment and Society*, 23/1 (2009): 142–59.

45. May et al.: *The British State and London's Migrant Division of Labour*.

Further Reading

Anderson, B. and Ruhs, M. 'Migrant Workers: Who Needs Them? A Framework for the Analysis of Staff Shortages, Immigration and Public Policy'. In M. Ruhs and B. Anderson (eds) *Who Needs*

Migrant Workers? Labour Shortages, Immigration and Public Policy. Oxford: Oxford University Press, 2010.

Beck, U. *Risk Society: Towards a New Modernity.* London: Sage, 1992.

Herzenberg, S. A., Alic, J. A. and Wial, H. *New Rules for a New Economy: Employment and Opportunity in Postindustrial America.* Ithaca and London: Cornell University Press, 2000.

Index

Note: *n* attached to a page number denotes an endnote

A

Accession 8 *see* New Member States
    (NMS/A8)
ageing
    and the welfare state 16–17, 136
    see also care sector
agency workers 99–100, 187–8
agriculture 88, 98, 145, 194
Alesina, Alberto 23–4
amnesties 81, 87–8, 146, 147, 148–9
asylum seekers 22

B

Baltic states 33–4, 39, 40
Banting, K. 20–1, 22, 23
Bay, A-H. 20
Belgium, posted workers 42
Blue Card system 2, 13*n*4
Bommes, M. 23

C

capitalism, varieties of (VoC) 107–9
care sector 125–42
    direct payments 128
    dominance of private sector 126–7
    funding pressures 125, 128, 135
    growing needs of 125, 136
    and immigration policy 129–30, 136
    importance of migrant labour 101,
        125, 131–4
    Italy 7, 84–6, 89–90
    poor wages and conditions 8–9, 127,
        132, 134–6
    in private households 128–9, 134–5,
        151–2, 153

research interviews 130–1
    Southern Europe 125, 150–1
    temporary workers 133
    vacancies and turnover 127
    work permits 129, 133
casual labour 12
construction industry 7–8, 42, 81–2,
    101, 192
coordinated market economies (CMEs)
    107–8, 109
Crepaz, M. 20

D

Danish family migration 159–84
    24-year rule 161
    2002 policies 160–7
    application fees 167, 169, 178
    application numbers 163–5, 168–9
    economic considerations 174–8
    effect on marriage partners 165–6
    financial guarantee 162, 167, 178
    human rights concerns 10, 160,
        169–72, 177, 178–9
    integration requirements 167, 168,
        174, 177
    language skills 168, 169, 170, 177
    marriage requirements 161–2,
        172, 176
    and move to Sweden 166–7
    points-based requirements 9,
        168, 171
    policy changes 9–10, 160–2,
        167–9, 178
    potential bias against Danish citizens
        10, 171–2, 179

Danish family migration (*Continued*)
   resident-partner conditions 161–2, 168
   rising marriage age 163, 165
   and welfare system 9–10, 159–60, 172–5
Denmark, posted workers 42
deportations 148, 153, 196

E

economic crisis 1, 34, 40, 43–4, 105
emerging market economies (EMEs) 107–8, 109
employer associations 107–113, 116–17
employers
   preference for migrant labour 98–100, 102, 197
   sanctions for employing illegal workers 152–4, 186, 196
   sponsorship of migrants 2, 9, 147, 151, 192–3, 198
   and workers' rights 11, 195–6
employment
   and British labour force 185
   labour and skills shortages 96–7, 102
   migrants' vulnerability 195–8
   posted workers 6, 37, 41–3, 48
   self-employment 192
   temporary employment 43–4, 133, 151, 188–9
   see also labour market; precarious employment
employment agencies 99–100, 187–8
employment protection 11
ethnic advocacy groups 106
European Convention on Human Rights 169–70
European Court of Justice (CJEU) 37, 41, 48, 52*n18*
European Union
   Blue Card system 2, 13*n4*
   dual migration system 4, 14*n8*
   economic convergence 45
   enlargement 33–4, 37

free movement regulations 5–6, 36, 46–7
   intro-EU mobility mixed effects of 35
   Maastricht Social Protocol 36–7
   migrant worker flows 38–41
   sanctions against employers of illegal migrants 152–4
   third-country nationals 13*n7*
   see also New Member States (NMS/A8)

F

family migration
   UK 191
   and welfare states 159–60
   see also Danish family migration
financial crisis 1, 34, 40, 43–4, 105
Finland, posted workers 42
France
   immigration policy 109–110, 116
   and underground economy 152
   work permits 109, 110
Freeman, Gary 105, 106
   Migration and the Political Economy of the Welfare State 4–5, 15–26

G

Geddes, A. 21, 23
Germany
   employer preferences 110–12, 116
   immigration policy 110–12
   IT green card initiative 111
   migrant inflows 39, 44
   posted workers 42
   skilled migrants 8, 111–12
   work permits 111, 112
Glaeser, E. 23–4

H

human rights 10, 11, 160, 169–72, 177, 178–9, 195–6

I

illegal immigration *see* irregular immigration
immigration controls 186, 190–2

industrial relations 41, 44, 48–9, 107
   see also trade unions
information technology 109, 111
Iraq, migrants 163, 165*f*
Ireland, migrant inflows 39
irregular immigration 143–57
   amnesties/regularisations 81, 87–8,
      146, 147, 148–9
   and deportations 146, 148, 153
   effects of 144–5
   measures to combat 150–5
   and over-stayers 195
   role of the state 196–8
   and sanctions against employers
      152–4, 186, 196
   sectors of employment 145
   and smugglers 147
   and social networks 147
   UK 10
   voluntary return incentives 148
   and vulnerability 195–8
   see also precarious employment
Italy 77–94
   amnesty programmes 81, 87–8, 149
   construction sector 81–2
   domestic and care migrant workers 7,
      84–6, 89–90
   economy 79, 80
   employment rates 79
   EU migrants 78, 79
   illegal immigrants 77–8, 86, 87,
      88–9, 90
   immigration policy 77–8, 86–91
   limited welfare services 83
   low-skilled workers 7, 11, 79–80, 81
   migrant inflows 39, 78–9
   pensions 82–3
   refugees 91*n*3
   segmented labour markets 12
   women migrants 79
   women's employment 7
   work visas 79, 86, 89

J
Johnston, R. 23

L
labour inspections 152–3
labour market
   alternatives to migrant labour 100–1
   effect of EU enlargement 45
   enforcement of legislation 151–4
   grey economy 186
   Norway 6, 61, 64–6, 71
   social models 3
   see also employment; underground
      economy; wages
language skills
   Denmark 168, 169, 170, 177
   Germany 112
   Norway 11, 63
   UK 99, 188
Latvia, wage rises 45
Laval Quartet decision 37, 41, 48, 52*n*18
liberal market economies (LME)
      107–8, 109
low-skilled migrants
   A8 (new EU member states) 188–9
   Italy 7, 11, 79–80, 81
   Norway 7, 72, 73–4
   recruitment problems 9, 147, 151
   temporary job search permits 151
   UK 8, 10

M
Maastricht Treaty, Social Protocol 36
mixed market economies (MMEs)
      107–8, 109

N
Netherlands, posted workers 42
networks 99, 147, 191, 192
New Member States (NMS/A8)
   care sector workers 130, 136
   construction industry 192
   and low-waged work 188–9
   migrant worker statistics 38–41
   numbers to UK 186–7
   skilled emigrants and human
      resources drain 35, 40, 45–6
Nicole-Drancourt, C. 189

Norway 59–76
  benefits exports 67, 71, 73
  disability pension 68
  EU citizens' access 62–3
  family benefits 63, 68
  immigration policy 60–1, 70–1
  Introduction programme 63, 73
  labour market 6, 61, 64–6, 71
  language and vocational training
      11, 63
  lone parent benefit 68
  low-skilled migrants 7, 72, 73–4
  migrants' use of social benefits 66–9
  Polish migrants 40–1
  posted workers 42
  refugees 62, 63
  social assistance programme 63, 67–8
  social benefits 62–4, 66–9
  Somali women 68
  'two track' welfare 69–70, 72
  Welfare and Migration Committee
      61–2, 70–4
  welfare system 6, 59–60

O

Onasuch, E. 20

P

Pedersen, A. 20
Piore, M.J. 188, 189, 190, 191
points-based systems
  Denmark 9, 168, 171
  Germany 112
  UK 2, 10, 113, 136, 186–7
Poland
  emigrants 34, 38–9, 40–1
  employer preferences 114, 115, 116
  employment rates 45
  illegal immigration 115
  immigration policy 114–16
  migrants into 115
  unemployment 34
  work permits 115
political economy, and employer
      preferences 107–9

posted workers 6, 37, 41–3, 48
precarious employment 187–9, 197–8
  see also irregular immigration;
      underground economy
public opinion 1, 17–18, 19–20, 22,
      23–4

R

refugees 62, 63, 91*n3*, 171
right-wing parties 18, 70, 105,
      173, 174
rights *see* human rights
Romania, emigrants 38–9

S

Sacerdote, B. 23
Sanderson, S. 30
Sarkozy II Law 110
shipyards 42
skilled migrants
  A8 (new EU member states) 40, 45–6
  France 110
  Germany 8, 111–12
  loss to sending state 35, 40, 45–6
  in low-waged jobs 99
  UK 113
skills
  measurement of 96–7, 102
  soft skills 97
  see also low-skilled migrants;
      points-based systems; skilled
      migrants
Smith, Jacqui 191
social care *see* care sector
social networks 147, 191
social policy 20–6
social security 36, 41–2, 49–50
social tourism 46, 49
Somali women, in Norway 68
Somalia, migrants 163, 164*f*
Soroka, S. 23
Southern Europe
  care services 125, 150–1
  emigration 44–5
  guestworker schemes 187

mixed market economies (MMEs)
107–8, 109
see also irregular immigration; Italy;
Spain
Spain
amnesty programmes 149
migrant inflows 39
students 133, 194
Sweden, Danish migrants 166–7
Switzerland, posted workers 42

T
Taylor-Gooby, P. 24
temporary employment 43–4, 133,
151, 188–9
Thailand, migrants 163, 164*f*
third-country nationals 2, 4, 13*n*7, 130,
136, 192–4
trade unions 3, 11–12, 38, 48–9, 105
training 8, 101, 107–8
Turkey, migrants 163, 164*f*, 166

U
underground economy 143–4, 145–6,
150–5
see also irregular immigration
United Kingdom
agricultural sector 98
care sector *see* care sector
construction sector 101
deportations 196
employer preferences 112–13, 116
Highly Skilled Migrants Programme
(HSMP) 113
immigration categories (tiers) 10,
113, 187, 191–2
immigration policy 102–3, 112–14,
136, 186–7
low-skilled migrants 8, 10
migrant inflows 39
migrant networks 99, 192
Migration Advisory Committee 114
points-based system 2, 10, 113, 136,
186–7
posted workers 42

rights of immigrants 11
social security 8
students 191
vocational training 8
work permits 114, 129, 130, 191,
193–4
Worker Registration Scheme (WRS)
130, 136, 186, 188–9
United Nations, conventions 170
United States 15, 17, 18, 19, 24

V
van der Waal, J. 20
vocational training 8, 101, 107–8

W
wages
care sector 8–9, 132, 134–5
downward influence of migrants 4,
18, 36
EU convergence 45
low wages for A8 migrants 188
minimum wage enforcement 190
minimum wages 11, 38, 48
skilled migrants in low-pay jobs 99
welfare programmes, expenditure
23–4
welfare states
and ageing 16–17
and business costs 16
establishment before immigrants'
arrival 21
and family migration 159–60
goals 16
and immigration 21–6
see also social policy
work permits
care sector 129, 133
France 109, 110
Germany 111, 112
Poland 115
UK 114, 129, 130, 133, 191, 193–4
Worker Registration Scheme (WRS)
130, 136, 186, 188–9
working holidaymakers 191, 194